Premier of Queensland
and Minister for Trade

Success is spelt SARINA

It is no surprise that Sarina Russo has chosen to become the author of a motivational biography.

This is after all the work of a woman dedicated to achievement and success.

That individual success is built from the tough times of the migrant kid through to a glamorous woman sharing centre stage with Presidents and Prime Ministers.

In life we all need people around us who exemplify that through hard work, dedication and a goal-focused drive the seemingly unachievable become reality. That is Sarina.

Apart from being rightly recognised locally, nationally and internationally as a pioneer and a woman making great things happen she is a wonderful role model for others – especially young women.

Peter Beattie MP
Premier and Minister for Trade

Executive Building
100 George Street Brisbane
PO Box 185 Brisbane Albert Street
Queensland 4002 Australia

Telephone +61 7 3224 4500
Facsimile +61 7 3221 3631
Email ThePremier@premiers.qld.gov.au
Website www.thepremier.qld.gov.au

Hi Mo,   *14/5/2004*

MEET ME
at the top!

I want to spend more time with you, when we next

The story of Sarina Russo, who started with nothing, made it
big in business, and now dines with Premiers and Presidents

meet in London!

love Yu,

Sarina Russo
with Russ Gleeson

Your so Special

crowncontent

Published by
Crown Content
A.C.N. 096 393 636
A.B.N. 37 096 393 636
Level 1, 141 Capel Street
Nth Melbourne Vic 3051
Telephone: (03) 9329 9800
Fax: (03) 9329 9698
Internet: www.crowncontent.com.au
Email: mail@crowncontent.com.au

The National Library of Australia
Cataloguing-in-Publication entry:

Russo, Sarina.
  Meet me at the top! : the story of Sarina Russo, who
  started with nothing, made it big in business, and now
  dines with premiers and presidents.

  ISBN 1 86350 380 3.

  1. Russo, Sarina. 2. Businesswomen - Australia - Biography.
  I. Gleeson, Russ, 1934- . II. Title.

338.761651374092

Cover and Text Design: Ben Graham
Cover Photo: Richard De Chezal

Printed in Australia by BPA Books

I Believe

I believe anyone can achieve success by following this simple seven-step rule:

1. Accept accountability and responsibility for your life.

2. Work harder on yourself than on your job.

3. Never stop learning.

4. Set yourself short-term and long-term goals.

5. Visualise yourself reaching a goal so clearly that you can taste your success.

6. Persist. Never give up.

7. Above all, **believe in yourself** with passion. Never waver in that belief and never falter in that passion.

I had the thrill of being at Wimbledon to see young Australian Lleyton Hewitt win the 2002 men's singles tennis title. To me he looked like a skinny kid an Italian mother would force-feed with pasta to build him up. David Nalbandian, his Argentinean opponent was taller and heavier. He looked stronger.

But as he began to play, the skinny kid exploded. Lleyton Hewitt suddenly seemed twice the size. He was a fury of action out there, but he was also calm and focused as he served. Determination was written all over his face. His self-belief was awesome. The crowd could feel it and his opponent seemed to shrink under its force.

Being at that game and seeing that demonstration of overpowering self-belief reinforced my own certainty that we can do anything if we set out minds to it. Follow your dream and believe in your dream.

Sitting just two rows in front of me that day was a living example of someone who had followed a dream to greatness, Sir Paul McCartney, the kid who came out of the back streets of Liverpool to become one of the world's greatest musicians. With him was his new bride Heather Mills. I called, *'Australia congratulates you, Sir Paul'* and he turned and gave me a wink. After the game we ran into each other on the stairway and I told Heather how much I had enjoyed watching her interview with Larry King on CNN. As we parted I gave Sir Paul a kiss on the cheek.

Sir Paul modestly says of his success, 'I was very, very lucky, and I worked very hard, so that's what brought money and fame'.

And that is so very true. We all need some luck. I was also at Wimbledon in 2001 and saw Goran Ivanisevic play Pat Rafter in the men's final. Rafter was near the top of world rankings and was favoured to win. Ivanisevic was ranked way down at 125 and was expected to lose. He had a history of erratic performances.

But as Ivanisevic explained later that day, he had a dream. He had visualised himself holding the Wimbledon trophy aloft – and that afternoon he brought that dream to life. He was at the brink of defeat twice in the fifth and final set but then, in an amazing turnaround, he snatched victory from the Australian champion. He got the luck. And he held the Wimbledon trophy aloft for the world to see.

It was his day. Rafter gave his all, but on this day it just wasn't enough. And there's a lesson in that.

You can't realise your dream every time. But you have to keep going for it. We saw an example of that in the 2002 US Men's Open, in which Pete Sampras, a past champion on a long losing streak, fought his way into the final for a match with Andre Agassi, who had eliminated Hewitt.

Sampras had been a loser in 33 tournaments in the previous two years.

But he kept going for his dream of winning just one more major. And it happened.

He defeated Agassi and at 31 became the oldest player to win the US Open for 32 years. It was his fifth US Open and first tournament win after a two-year drought.

For those who discover the power of self-belief, I believe life is a pathway of opportunities.

We all have the potential to make a difference, no matter who our parents are and no matter whether they are rich or poor. The power to make that difference does not come from what we hold, or where we're from. It comes from what we have in our minds and in our hearts, and from the determination we use to pursue our goals.

Accept who you are today, in pursuit of what you want to be tomorrow. Your future begins the moment you set yourself a goal with these words: **I can... I will.**

I have a plaque on my desk that reads: *It can be done.* That is the philosophy that has guided my life. See you at the top.

Sarina Russo

Acknowledgements

This book is written in the first person, the standard writing technique for books such as this, because it enables a narrative that is simple, direct and to the point. As a committed advocate of clear communication I felt obliged to go along with the publisher's wishes in that respect, but I want to make it plain that the continuous use of the 'I' word does not mean I have forgotten or overlooked the many people who have had influential roles in my personal development and the growth of the Sarina Russo Group of companies. I have cause to be grateful to many people I have encountered in my life's journey, people who have worked alongside me and people who have supported me, encouraged me and inspired me. My gratitude extends to those who may have put obstacles in my way or opposed me. I say this because the great lesson in my life is that adversity simply means you must regroup, rethink and try again. If your idea is right, your focus is clear and your motives are good, you will succeed.

Nothing in this life is more important than family ... and friends. I was fortunate to be born into a family that lived and worked as a unit. That tradition has carried on. We laugh, we cry – and yes, we sometimes disagree, because we are passionate people, but always we come back to one another. I would like to acknowledge my mother Maria for her strength and courage and my sisters Rita and Rosina and my brother Joe for always being there when the chips were down. I am proud of my nephews, nieces and great nieces, all beautiful young people, whose growth and development I follow with deep affection and whose love and support I cherish.

I would especially like to thank my brother-in-law Gerardo Pennisi who has been a pillar of strength and a mentor to me throughout my business life. I could never have got where I have without his presence in the business and the wisdom, advice and guidance he has imparted. To my nephews Mark Berlese, Marcello and Andrew Pennisi and nieces Angela and Maria Berlese, who work with me in our business, I extend my thanks for their talent, their vigour, their enthusiasm and their commitment.

I must also recognise my nephew David Pennisi whose creative architectural skill and advice has been crucial to our property rejuvenation and modernisation strategy.

There are many people who have played pivotal roles in the development of the Sarina Russo Group of companies, from the early days of my first business, 'The Office' Business Academy, through to the development of the Russo Institute of Technology and Sarina Russo Job Access network. At the head of this list I must place Janet Vallino, who got me my first job as an evening typing teacher, opening up a wonderful future for me. I have enjoyed the long term support of wonderful, talented staff, including Diane O'Neill who was with me from the early days and remained with me for 13 years, Roslyn Francke, whose loyalty kept her with me for 22 years, Katherine Nunn, who is still with us after 15 years and former staff members Stephanie Butcher, Maria Minasi, Julie Massey, Robin Foster, each of whom gave me 15 years of service.

I have been fortunate to have benefited from the services of gifted managers, particularly Kevin Ayre, general manager of Sarina Russo Job Access and Michael Barnes, General Manager of the Russo Institute of Technology, whose loyalty and dedication to our business has been utterly outstanding. I would also like to acknowledge the excellent contributions of former managers Dudley Martin and John Slater who moved on to new opportunities and have my blessing.

I cannot overlook Michael Wayland, of Sydney, who coached me on the dynamics and strategies of financial accountability in our business. Thank you, Michael.

Paul Anderson, of the National Australia Bank, holds a special place in my list of people to whom I owe a debt of gratitude for showing faith in my ability to run a profitable business. Also on that list of special people is Brian White, who defied the odds and nominated me as the first Queensland female member of the Young Presidents' Organisation.

Outside of my business there are many other people in my life to whom I owe a debt of gratitude, close friends, including boyfriends, with whom I can unwind, joke and laugh and who have touched my life in such a positive way. They know who they are and how important they are in my life. I cherish their friendship.

The credit for the clever diagrams that illustrate a number of chapters in this book must go to my nephew Marcello Pennisi, who also put together the business and family photographs we have used. I thank Marcello for his dedication to this project and for his patience and attention to detail in checking the manuscript.

A note to my indefatigable co-author

You have now manifested a lifelong goal to create a book in order to share my experiences and lessons. Thank you for making our vision come true.

A note to all the bosses who fired me

To all the bosses who fired me, or 'coached me out' through lack of opportunity – namely Mark Varley, David McEachern, George Deeb, Ross Clarke, Harold Lowes, Ian Richardson and many others – I also say thank you. I may not have been where I am today had you not, by your actions, strengthened my resolve to find financial independence. That stage of my life was a learning curve. In retrospect I am grateful for the lessons I received in all of your businesses.

Dedication

I dedicate this book to all the people in our businesses who have contributed so richly to our success; to the management and teachers of the Russo Institute of Technology whose commitment and guidance has opened new doors for the thousands of students who have completed our courses; to the students themselves who have gone forward with the qualifications to build brilliant careers; to the staff at our Sarina Russo Job Access agencies who have brought new hope to the lives of thousands of unemployed; to the job search candidates who have used our services with success; and to the employers who have demonstrated faith in our abilities by giving jobs to our students and job search candidates.

Bali – In Memoriam

As we were putting the finishing touches to this book, unknown terrorists staged a bomb attack on throngs of tourists who were out for a night of fun at Kuta Beach in Bali. Many Australians were among those who died in that outrage. Many Australians were among those who were terribly wounded. My heart goes out to the families of the dead. Australia prays that they can find some way to come to terms with their tragic loss. We pray for the speedy recovery of the wounded, not only from their terrible physical injuries but also from the shocking mental trauma they have experienced. Terrorism is an evil we must all join together to eradicate, not only by force but by making greater effort to share with poor, underprivileged and dispossessed societies of the world and by being tolerant of cultures that are different from our own. I commend the peace message of President Bill Clinton I have written about in this book.

Contents

Introduction

It is a lovely, balmy night in Brisbane – Friday, March 1, 2002 – and a never-ending procession of limousines, taxis and private cars is dropping off passengers at one of the city's swankiest hotels, the Sheraton.

To the passer-by, this activity is obviously the prelude to some grand event involving the city's VIPs.

In gorgeous evening gowns and immaculate dinner suits, they arrive in their hundreds and make their way to the hotel's grand ballroom which has been transformed into a giant dining hall.

There is a hubbub of voices and an air of expectancy as the last of the 750 guests take their seats at their assigned tables. Then a sudden hush as the double doors to the giant hall open. A voice booms out over the public address system: *Ladies and gentlemen, please welcome the 42nd President of the United States, Mr Bill Clinton ...*

The 750 guests rise to their feet and the room erupts into deafening applause. The announcement continues ....

'... with Sarina Russo.'

The President walks through this applauding throng to the central dining table. At his side is a woman in a glittering silver lamé evening gown. Me, Sarina Russo.

We take our seats, side by side at a table of 18 others including the Queensland Premier Peter Beattie and Brisbane's Lord Mayor Jim Soorley, and the night begins, with the highlight to be an address by the President himself about terrorism, about forging peace and about closing the gap between the haves and the have-nots of the world.

And it was to be my task to deliver an address of welcome to him.

Me, making an entrance with a US President? Me, representing the city of Brisbane? Me, hosting this grand event as CEO of my companies, the Sarina Russo Group, which had bought the naming rights (available to the company that put in the closest bid to $110,000) as a service to the city and in support of a children's charity? In my wildest dreams I could never have imagined this happening.

I was the kid from the working class side of the tracks, the kid who came to Spring Hill, Brisbane as a five-year-old from Sicily, the kid whose migrant Dad was a bridge worker and carpenter, the kid who couldn't speak English, the kid who was scorned at primary school because she ate parmesan cheese and salami sandwiches, the young woman who was fired from several jobs after leaving school (and failing junior and senior English exams).

But I was also the kid who started a one-room typing school and grew it into the Russo Institute of Technology, teaching English and business courses to students from all over Australia and around the world. And I was the kid who grew the job-finding office I started for my students into a three-state network finding jobs for thousands of Australian unemployed in partnership with the Federal Government.

But is this description of my evening with a US President really worth the opening chapter of a book? Is it an exercise in vanity?

My answer is 'yes' to the first question and 'no' to the second. Let me tell you why. As a young woman leaving school I did not want to be a failure, but that seemed to be the direction I was heading, losing job after job.

One traumatic day I found myself jobless again, desperately shouting at my tear-streaked image in my bedroom mirror, *'I'll do it or die'*. The dismissal I had experienced earlier that day had been outrageously unfair. I was furious.

My fury awoke a determination to turn my life around, no matter what it took. And that's how I discovered I had a talent.

The one thing I was really good at was typing. I scraped up enough money ($2600) to start a small typing and secretarial school in one rented room over a bank in Brisbane.

I began with just nine students who wanted to learn a skill that would get them a job.

I gave my school the grand name of 'The Office' Business Academy.

I vowed to every student that I would get them a job. After all, I had as much experience at winning jobs as I had at losing them.

I told my students that if they really tried to be the best they could be at everything they did, they could reach any goal they set themselves. I told them that if they really believed in themselves, they would succeed. I taught them with music and with jokes and laughter because I believed you worked better and learned better when you were having fun.

I kept my promise. I always got them jobs and my school grew and grew and the courses I offered became more and more diversified.

And that was my talent – getting people to the starting line of a new phase in their lives, motivating them to believe in themselves, pushing them to set goals for themselves and to really go after them. I also discovered I was good at networking, which is how I got jobs for my students. I networked the business community mercilessly.

I've now been in the teaching and career launching business for more than 23 years. I intend to be in this business for as long as I am physically able, helping people to launch themselves into careers that will give them fulfilment in their lives.

I can never stop doing it because I get so much out of it. You've never lived until you've seen the faces of students light up with joy as you tell them you've got them a job interview – and even greater joy when they come back and tell you they've got the job and they're on the way to becoming financially independent.

People often come to you lacking in self-belief, with very little self-esteem and very little optimism or confidence because it's been drained out of them by continuous rejection.

To see the transformation when they've learned a skill, when they've discovered that someone does really care about their future, when they come to believe that they do have a particular talent, is enormously gratifying. More than that ... inspiring.

Nothing is greater than enhancing someone's life. In enhancing theirs you are enhancing your own.

And now here I am, writing a book. Why?

It's for them, for all the students, job seekers and anyone facing the challenge of making a new start in life. I want to show them it doesn't matter where you're from or how temporarily poor you may be. I want to show them it's not what happens to you that matters. What counts is what you do about it.

I want to show them you can turn adversity and setbacks into stepping stones to higher achievements, for that's what my life has been ... a journey of surmounting obstacles and rising above adversity. You don't say *'impossible'* to me and get away with it.

I want to show these people that if you really believe in yourself, anything is possible – just as it was for the Sicilian migrant child of struggling parents who grew up to become a businesswoman hosting an American President at a grand dinner in Brisbane on the night of March 1, 2002.

Just as it was for that same person who went to Paris a few weeks after that Clinton dinner to be inducted as one the world's leading women entrepreneurs for the Year 2002.

Yes, that was a grand event too and it was another experience that reinforced my belief that you can start with nothing and rise to the top if you believe in yourself, if you are willing to learn, if you work hard and if you're prepared to take some risks.

I didn't plan to create an institute of technology, or a national job access network – and I didn't plan to be chosen as one of the 40 leading women entrepreneurs in the world for 2002.

It just happened because I wanted to keep growing my business, to keep growing myself by constant learning and challenging myself to do more. Because I was always on the lookout for opportunities to improve my business, myself and my team.

And because I never took no for an answer when I needed to borrow money, or to introduce new courses to my business college before it became the Russo Institute of Technology.

It also happened because I was either very lucky or very good at recruiting talented, supportive staff. (My bank manager tells me I have a radar-like knack of recruiting the right people, but the truth is I like all people. I enjoy meeting people, no matter who they are. Everyone has something different to offer.)

As I made my entrance to the great hall of a grand castle at Chantilly near Paris, in late April 2002 to be inducted to the honour roll of the leading women entrepreneurs of the world for 2002 I couldn't stop thinking about what had got me there: the students who had inspired me to grow and grow and the staff who were the backbone of my businesses.

I have an amazing team of people working, not for me, but with me at all levels. We are in the success business, shooting for our own personal goals and revelling in the successes of our students, our job search candidates and the employers who give them jobs.

As I took my place in the gathering of the rich and famous with other nominees at the Chateau de Montvillargenne at Chantilly for our induction I could not help thinking about the difficult times in my business career, the setbacks and the events that seemed like disasters at the time.

Now here I was living a fairytale that had come about because for every setback my business experienced, for every mini disaster, for every opportunity that needed seizing, there had been someone from among my staff who had stepped forward to help find a solution.

I was really here for them.

It was because of the impetus they had given me with their support that my name and profile had gone before an International Selection Committee of the Leading Women Entrepreneurs of the World movement to be considered for appointment to their honour roll for 2002.

Hundreds of names had been submitted to the committee by business leaders and women's organisations in 68 countries and were drawn from the databases of universities, libraries, and major consulates spanning 72 countries. Only 40 were chosen to join the honour roll for the year 2002.

In recognition of our induction to the honour roll, each of us was presented with an exquisitely designed white gold gingko leaf pin displaying a gloriously beautiful Paspaley (Australia) South Sea Pearl.

The leading women entrepreneurs of the world movement was founded in 1997 by Anita Roberts, President and Chief Executive Officer of the Star Group, a major public relations organisation in the US, and is now supported by Harvard University's John F. Kennedy School of Government, Fortune Magazine, United Airlines and many other organisations.

The Paris ceremony was the sixth annual event, with 280 women now having been inducted as leading women entrepreneurs of the world. Collectively, they contribute more than $100 billion to the global economy.

When she founded the movement, Anita Roberts had this vision: to create a sisterhood of the most powerful and influential women on earth to act as a force for good.

She pledged the new movement's support for the Feed the Children organisation which provides food for a million people a day in 45 countries.

Now as a member of this sisterhood, I have been invited to participate in Harvard University's global program entitled Women and Power: Leadership in a New World.

This movement incorporates the university's Women Waging Peace, Women World Leaders and Women's Leadership Board programs.

Anita Roberts told us at the Paris ceremony in April 2002: 'In this world utterly trembling from terrorism now, I can ideally foresee all of you Leading Women Entrepreneurs of the World waging peace in each of your countries. There are now 280 of you in over 60 countries.

'Each of you must mobilise all the women and resources in your own country. We want peace in this world – and the leading women entrepreneurs of the world can be the peacemakers.'

I feel good about having been inducted into her sisterhood and I am grateful for the opportunity to make some contribution to her cause. Sadly she died of cancer a few months after the Paris awards ceremony, but the flame of her vision and her cause still burns.

The future of the world lies with our young people. They will be the leaders of tomorrow. They will make good leaders, wise leaders tomorrow if they are given opportunities today to develop themselves through learning and experience in the workplace.

I hope this story of my experiences of failure and success will encourage, inspire and motivate you now more than ever to make the best of yourself you possibly can.

The Lessons

As an educator I believe in using repetition to reinforce the lessons in what we read and in what we experience. These are the key lessons I would like you to take from what I have written in this introduction:

1. Take responsibility for your life and be accountable.

2. Believe in yourself with passion and you will find success.

3. You will learn better if you can learn while having fun.

4. You can turn adversity and setbacks into stepping stones to higher achievements.

5. Never accept '*impossible*' for an answer.

6. Set your goals – anything is possible if you really believe in yourself.

Part One

CHAPTER ONE

The dutiful daughter – in a culture trap

I am proud to say that I was born in Sicily, in the town of Castiglione di Sicilia, which, in English, means Castle of the Lion of Sicily. Castiglione sits on the north-western slopes of Mt Etna, that rumbling volcanic mountain so beloved by vulcanologists because it periodically puts on a show for them, belching smoke and the occasional gush of molten lava. Some say there is a correlation between the volcanic nature of my birthplace and my passion for life. Many other successful Sicilians around the world could say the same because they, too, have passionate natures.

Castiglione, which is on a knoll and out of the path of lava flows, can trace its origins back almost 3000 years. We know this through an amazing ruin that stands above the town and has been dated by archaeologists. It is a Greek fortress hewn out of solid rock by the Greeks who set up a colony known as Naxos in Sicily in 735 BC.

Nearby are the remains of a Norman Castle built 1300 years later in 1100 AD. For those of us who were born there, the history of civilisation runs through our veins. The Greeks, the Carthaginians, the Romans, the Normans, the French, the Spanish, the Austrians have all fought over this island of my birth, conquered it and impregnated it with their seed.

When you think of Sicily, don't just think of peasants and Mafia. Today law enforcement authorities there are working with brave determination to drive out the Mafia.

Archimedes, the great Greek mathematician and inventor, was a Sicilian. He was born there in 287 BC, postulated his theory of hydrostatics there (a body in fluid loses weight equal to the weight of the amount of fluid it displaces) and died there, slain by a Roman soldier who found him drawing a mathematical diagram in the sand and took offence when Archimedes told him, 'do not disturb my diagrams'.

Archimedes knew the risk he was taking. The Roman army had just overrun and conquered his home city of Syracuse. But for him, life was not worth living unless he had the freedom to pursue his life-long work in mathematics.

What price freedom? ... to do as you want to do ... to be as you want to be? Little did the Roman soldier who stopped Archimedes's heart with his sword thrust know that he had failed to kill his victim. Archimedes still lives and will live forever, not just for his theory of hydrostatics – the Archimedes principal – but for many other mathematical and geometric theories as well.

The desire for freedom comes in many guises. As for me, I have been prepared to pay any price to achieve it, as I will explain later.

We Sicilians are a people of passion, we are proud, we are loyal, we are opportunists, hard workers and realists. As some hardy flowers will grow through cracks in concrete, so do we have the capacity to bloom in the harshest environments. We are survivors.

My father Antonino was the elder of the two sons and two daughters of a farmer who grew grapes and hazelnuts on fields below the village of Castiglione. When Antonino married my mother, Maria, he moved into her parents' home in the town because there was no room in his father's small house.

My mother's house is at least 450 years old, rising three stories, which makes it sound grand but it was not. Trust me, there were no mod cons. It was very narrow and if you were to make room for a growing family, the only way to go was up.

Four children were born to my mother in that house: first, my sister Rosina, then my brother Joe, then my sister Rita and finally me. I was christened Rosaria, but everyone called me Sarina and the name has stuck. I like it.

When I was a year old my father left Castiglione, where there was no work for him, except on his father's farm.

Through village gossip he had heard about a new land of opportunity called Australia.

A man who was prepared to work hard could buy property there and build a future for his family.

There was plenty of work for good wages, it was said, and the land was cheap. What more could a man want, especially if he had muscles of iron, like my father, with a determination and fierce will to match? Besides, my father had already had his eyes opened to the wider world. As a younger man he had been recruited into the Italian army and served in North Africa.

He was a prisoner of war there and later was also prisoner of war in England where, like many other Italian POWs, he was billeted out with a rural family to help run their farm.

So in 1952 he joined the migrant stream that was draining Castiglione and many other parts of Sicily of its young male blood and sailed for Brisbane, leaving us behind until he established a home for us to come to. In Castiglione today, incidentally, about 80 percent of the villagers either do not work because there is no work for them or they are retired. All the jobs that are available are taken by the remaining 20 per cent, mostly the young people.

Four years went by, four years of letters and money in the mail and I forgot what my father looked like. It may have been different if there had been a telephone, at least I would have had a voice to connect him to, but there were no phones in our house.

When he sent us his command to join him in 1956, I was five years old and confused about what was happening.

I remember I was sad to be leaving behind my aunts and uncles and cousins. Today my cousin by marriage, Salvatore Barbagello is the Mayor of Castiglione.

I can remember that when our ship docked in Brisbane and this big man with a moustache and a hat met us and embraced us I was alarmed. Who was this man?

He paid a lot of attention to me, the youngest. My brother and sisters were not the mystery I was to him because they had formed their personalities before he left us. They had memories of him and he of them. They knew who he was, they knew he had to be obeyed.

I had no memories of him and he had few, if any, of me because I was so small when he left. I did not know that when this man spoke, his word was absolute law. But I soon learned that this was so.

He took us to a house he had bought in Wickham Terrace, Spring Hill, Brisbane, which was in the tough end of town. He had partitioned it so that he could rent some of it out. We lived in one half and two other families lived in the other half which had been divided into separate living areas with a shared bathroom.

I was enrolled at the St Stephen's and then All Hallows schools where the nuns struggled to teach this new Italian migrant child how to speak, read and write English.

Being younger and not as deeply programmed in the Sicilian dialect as my older sisters and brother, I picked up conversational English quicker than them. Because of this I became the family's 'translator' at an early age.

We lived a life of hard work and no frills. During the week my father did his job as a bridge carpenter and leading hand on the Hornibrook Highway and at weekends he farmed a banana plantation he had leased at Upper Brookfield, which was then a rural area outside Brisbane, but today is a settled suburb of the city.

My mother worked during the week in the Golden Circle Pineapple Cannery and somehow found the time and energy to carry out all the cooking, sewing and housework that was necessary to keep a family well fed and in reasonable comfort.

At weekends my father would take us all, wife and four children, to the banana plantation and put everyone, except me, to work; planting bananas, picking bananas, packing bananas, cultivating and so on. I was too small at five years of age to do any work. But not too small to have great fun sliding down hills on large banana leaves with my sister Rita.

Joe and Rosina got jobs. They brought all of their wages home to my father, who gave them back a small amount for pocket money and put the rest in the 'family fund' which was where my mother's cannery earnings went as well. So did the rent from the two other families that shared our house.

The fact that Joe and Rosina had jobs did not get them out of the weekend at the banana plantation. They would never have dared to protest. You did not question my father.

When I was 10 years of age, the 'family fund' had enough in it to buy a small vineyard at Wacol and a block of three rental flats (apartments) in Petrie Terrace, Brisbane. Dad gave up the lease on the banana plantation.

If I had thought life was hard before this, I was about to discover that it had only been a gentle warm-up.

Because of my father's trust in me as his translator/interpreter and mouthpiece, I got the job of managing the flats and the farm.

I started doing this when I was a 10-year-old school kid, sprucing up the flats, advertising them, meeting the prospective tenants, setting the rent and collecting the rent.

My sister Rita helped me with the heavy work like painting the walls, but I was the supervisor which Rita resented, because she was older than me and felt she should have been the chosen one. Whenever tenants had a complaint they came to me. It was my responsibility to deal with it.

At weekends my father would take us all out to the vineyard at Wacol to labour in the vineyard, planting vines, pruning, spraying, tying, weeding, picking, packing.

If there had been a contest to find the smallest kid in Australia with the most experience at shovelling, I would have won it hands down. From all the hours I spent at the end of a shovel I certainly worked out what it was I didn't want to do in life.

The years rolled on. First Rosina got married (to a wonderful Italian man named Ricardo) and then my brother Joe also married (to a beautiful Italian girl named Maria.) Their departures brought more work for Rita and me.

My father leaned on me for everything, negotiating prices for the table grapes from the vineyard, dealing with the produce market buyers and vendors – even evictions and his tax returns. I had to get all the figures together and put them in order for the accountant.

If a tenant missed paying the rent he would tell me I must evict him or her. There was one tenant who had not paid for two weeks. I knocked on the door and this tall, handsome university student opened it. I looked up at him and told him that if he did not pay the rent he would have to leave.

He looked down at me. Then he looked at the man standing behind me, a man with a pencil thin moustache and black eyes that glittered at him from beneath a hat. My father had the Sicilian look, the look you might associate with the Mafiosi, though he was into no such thing. But the look was enough.

'I'll get the money,' the tall tenant said. And he did.

My determination to make something of my life, to one day win freedom, financial independence and respect was forged in those years, not only because of my feelings of being enslaved by my family duties, but also because of the way we migrant children were regarded in the community.

Just up the street from our humble Wickham Terrace home was a hotel-motel that had two features of great appeal to us as children. One was a swimming pool and the other was a laneway down one side of it. This provided a great shortcut to school.

This establishment must have been very profitable because the owner drove a Rolls-Royce.

But he was not a tolerant or sympathetic man. One hot day he caught us looking longingly over the fence at his pool and chased us away. Then he caught us in the laneway and forbade us to use it ever again.

Across the street lived two spinsters. They also were quite well-to-do – or at least they were well enough off to buy a television set when TV came to Australia in 1956.

We, of course, did not have a TV. My father refused to buy one, but the two spinsters across the street allowed Rita and me to watch their TV from their veranda, on the outside looking in.

There we were, me standing on a box because I was smaller than Rita, peering through the window at a small TV screen and straining to hear the sounds of *Bonanza* on a Friday night.

I felt marginalised by those experiences with the neighbours. They meant no harm but they were wary of us and we could sense it. Why they were wary, we did not know. We just felt that for some unknown reason we were not *'one of them'*.

It's funny, though, how the wheel turns. Many years later, first one son and then another son of the hotel owner came to me for help in finding employment.

I was delighted to help them, because by then I had formed my philosophy about negative experiences with people – *the best form of revenge is massive success*.

Rita left school after Grade 8 and became a hairdresser. School for me was a joy and a struggle. The joy in it was the escape from the dominating will of my father. The struggle was with English classes.

Unlike most other children I could not turn to my parents for help with my homework because they knew less about English than I did. I used to go to the homes of my neighbours asking for their help and in doing so I made a great discovery: whenever you have a problem don't be too proud to ask for help, for always there will be someone who will give that help.

I had a natural talent for figures and had no trouble with arithmetic – or conversational English – but the pure grammar aspects of English like subjects and predicates, tenses and cases, syntax, forms and structures, were too much for me.

I would have loved to have done my senior year at school but failed my Grade 10 Junior English. (The following year I repeated Grade 10 English at night school and passed it).

My Grade 10 nuns told me I wouldn't make it to senior. I left those gates, those sandstone gates, really feeling inadequate, totally disillusioned. The one thing I had been really good at was typing. I could do 60 words a minute faultlessly at school and worked up to 100 as an invoice typist.

But to me this was cold consolation because I knew it would doom me to a career as an invoice typist.

Of course there is nothing wrong with being a typist, but if I had the potential to do more then I wanted more. What, I did not know. All I knew was that I wanted more.

My father was very excited when I got my first job at the age of 17. It was as a typist with Dalgety Australia Limited. He said, '*carina (my dear little one) you've got a very, very secure job now*'. But despite that job he still made me work at the vineyard every weekend – and in holiday periods. I think I was the only girl in Brisbane who didn't like holidays, especially Christmas holidays because they meant I would be outside working some days in 40-degree heat picking and packing grapes. How stylish it is today to say that you are the owner of a vineyard!

I worked in the shipping department at Dalgety's and for a while I thought it was a great job. I used to have this massive typewriter for typing up manifests on huge sheets of paper.

Doing this every day gave me a pain in the neck. Today it's called RSI. After 18 months of this I used to look around and say to myself, I don't want to live like this, what can I do with my life? My father was taking my wages, for the 'family fund', and giving me back a small amount for pocket money. I felt I was going nowhere.

I was now out in the world and coming into contact with young men. I believe I was an attractive and extremely fit young lady (from all that hard work in the vineyard) with black hair and large, smouldering brown eyes.

I was constantly asked out on dates. My father would not hear of it, especially if it was an Australian boy – unless, of course, he had the intent to marry me.

Let me put my father into perspective. He was very Italian. He never went out without wearing his felt hat and I have to admit he looked a little bit like a Mafia Don. Just a glimpse of him would put the frighteners on any boy who came around to ask if he could take me out.

I was frightened of him myself. He would fly into a rage if any family member dared defy him. He was the master. And that was it. His word was law. Absolutely. We all grew up believing it.

He was a highly respected figure in the Italian community, the Sicilian community. They all loved him. He was very generous. He always used to help people out.

He was elegant and meticulous. If you ever opened his drawers – we still have them – everything was in perfect order. He was very organised. And I am like that too.

But he was locked in a time warp, rigidly ruled by Sicilian traditions which had to be followed without question or dissent. These traditions, all centred on preservation of family and one-ness of family, drove him, empowered him.

Daughters did not associate with men who had no intentions of marrying them. The family's honour demanded that the daughter go to her marriage bed a virgin, so to go out with a man who had not declared his intentions of marriage was an absolute no-no.

What he wanted was a situation in which a young man would have seen me, decided I was the girl he wanted to take for his wife, go to my father and tell him of his intentions and obtain my father's permission to take me out. The courtship, and the wedding plans, would proceed from there. My two sisters and my brother married in just that way.

It was impossible to convince him that I really just wanted to get to understand what dating was like. It was even more impossible to explain to him that in this country you went out on dates with guys until you met someone you fell in love with and then you waited until he proposed to you and you accepted. None of this arranged marriage stuff.

I was rescued from my job typing shipping manifests for Dalgetys by a woman friend who said she could get me a job with a firm named Evans Deakin as her husband's secretary.

I thought, Wow! ... from a manifest typist to secretary. And I am only 19. I like the sound of that. So I resigned. I told my Dad.

He was horrified – and angry. He said, 'you've given up a secure job?'

I said, 'yes Dad. I've given up a secure job. But now I'm going to be a secretary. Dad. A secretary. It's been my dream to be a secretary'.

He said, 'I don't want you to resign. Can you go back and tell them you are staying?'. I said, 'well no. I want to be this secretary.' He said, 'no I want you to go back. This is a very secure job. You're giving up a secure job'.

That was the Italian attitude for you: security is more important than personal development.

I lasted less than five weeks in that secretary's job before I was fired. I thought, how am I going to tell my Dad? I've got no job and none to go to. I thought, no I won't tell him. I'll just go and find another job. And I quickly did.

I applied for this job in a legal office. The first person I met was a good-looking guy. I thought, 'wow, great marriage material.'

He was the son of a senior partner. I thought, I'm going to do well here. Remember, my conditioning was that I had to be married and I was running out of time.

He said, 'can you do legal work?'.

'No,' I replied, 'but I'm willing to learn. I can do it. You can train me'.

He said, 'you've got the job'.

The next thing, he wanted to date me. I thought, 'wow, my dream's come true'. Then I realised, no, I can't date him. How can I tell Dad? He's going to say, 'it's only a date. There's no intention of marriage'.

So I lied to this good looking guy, 'no, I'm sorry, I'm already dating'.

I lost the job, but in the eight weeks I was there I gained knowledge of legal terminology that would serve me in good stead.

I thought, oh no, now what do I tell my Dad? I was sick in the stomach. I thought, how do I tell my Dad I'm no longer a secretary at Evans Deakin? I didn't want to tell him about this legal job I had just lost as well.

I decided I would find another legal job. And I did. I walked in for an interview in a brand new building, the best looking high-rise in the city. I was excited by the prospect of working in such an environment, dressing up and playing the significant role of valued legal secretary.

I could tell that the solicitor who interviewed me was impressed. When I told him I was looking for a job, he asked, 'do you know anything about legal work?'. I told him I did and I threw in all the legal terms I could remember about mortgage documents and contracts of sale.

He gave me the job, and at first I did ok. Then one day he said to me, 'bring your shorthand book and take down some dictation'.

I thought, oh my God. Shorthand! How do I do it?

One of the other secretaries could see that I was upset. She was a lovely girl and she was a great shorthand writer. She said to me, 'don't worry Sarina, I'll stand outside the door and I'll take down the dictation'. I was grateful, but I knew it was only a short term solution. What was I to do?

During that first session with my new friend outside the door, I kept on saying to the solicitor, 'could you speak louder please. I have an ear infection and I'm having trouble hearing you'.

In later sessions, taking down his flow of legal terminology myself, half in shorthand and half in spelt-out words. I really had no clue. I thought I'd better make a confession.

I found the strength to tell him, 'I really don't fit into this job'.

He said, 'no, you do. We'd like you to stay'.

I thought, wow! He wants me to stay. Isn't that exciting. Now I can tell my Dad I've got a real job. I was there for two years. Dad thought I was dating. Sometimes I would finish work at 11 o'clock at night. Dad would say, 'no way. No legal firm would keep you there until 11 o'clock at night'.

But it was the truth. This was during a period of booming land sales in the 1970s and we really were stretched to keep up with all the legal work. My boss would drop me off and I would be home at 11 o'clock. It was really hard. Finally, I just thought, what am I going to do? I really hate this job. I'm finding it exhausting. And my boss could tell I was no longer challenged or enthused. He suggested I work for a partner in the litigation department, but I didn't think that was prestigious enough for me and I didn't think I could cope with litigation terminology.

It was a bad time for me. A year earlier, Rita had married a wonderful Italian boy named Gerardo Pennisi, who was a solicitor – and whose family came from a town in Sicily not far from Castiglione. Perfect match.

Her marriage meant I was the only child at home – 19 years of age, with restricted freedom.

There was still the work at the vineyard every weekend and by now my father had bought another block of four flats at Highgate Hill, which also became my responsibility to manage. I had been able to save $2000 in a bank account and when my father asked me to lend it to him to help buy the apartments, I said yes – but it took him two years to repay me without any interest.

I was determined to break free. I enrolled at the Hubbard's night school as a mature age student at the age of 21 to study Year 12. It took me three tries to pass Year 12 English, but was I going to give up? Never! I was driven by the desire not only to improve myself but also to get out of the house and enjoy some company of my own age at night.

What a triumph it was to get that Year 12 pass because it was my passport to something I had always thought was beyond my dreams – university. At the age of 23 I was accepted into the arts faculty of the University of Queensland to study English and Australian politics. When that letter of acceptance came it was like winning a lottery. I showed the letter to my Dad and he was excited too – and so proud. A child of his, smart enough to go to university to study English and Australian politics? Fantastic!

In the meantime I had quit my job with the solicitor who wanted to transfer me to the litigation department and obtained a position with another legal firm – a brilliant job as legal secretary to a senior partner in a top firm. I was travelling!

My boss in this firm was campaigning as a political candidate for a seat in Federal Parliament.

I was a dedicated, committed legal secretary but I liked my boss so much I helped with his campaign. We worked hard, but he did not win the election.

One Friday my boss called me into his office. I thought it must be about a pay rise, but he said, 'DCM ... don't come Monday'. I was devastated. Absolutely devastated. I just could not understand that after two years of being so committed, I was being asked to leave.

I told my father and he said, 'I told you so. If you had stayed at that Dalgety's job you would have none of this'.

What do you tell an Italian father?

Next, I found a job as the secretary of a member of parliament and I thought, *this is it, this is for me*, but after about three months of doing very little, I actually rang my former boss who had given me the DCM and said, 'can I have my job back?'

He said, 'you never go backwards'. (In hindsight, what great advice that was.)

I said, 'no, no. I want your job'.

He said, 'no, you never go backwards, Sarina.'

I thought, now I'm stuck with this job, but after my 7th month, it was announced that the politician's seat was to be redistributed at the next election. Instead of keeping me there until the seat was redistributed, he recruited his fiancée. I lost my job. There were no unfair dismissal tribunals in those days.

This was a time of great misery in my life. I felt trapped by the pressures my father was putting on me, denying me any social life, running his real estate business and labouring at the vineyard every weekend. Believe me, this was not easy, especially in the summer, when you were picking grapes under blazing sun in heat of 100° Fahrenheit and more.

This was when I found the strength to leave home. I was determined to improve my life. After losing my job with the politician I got a job in another legal office, situated in the MLC building, one of Brisbane's tallest and finest. Through a friend, Janet Vallino, I also got a part time job teaching typing at night at a firm called Key Personnel.

I couldn't take it anymore. I had reached a crossroads. I had to get away. I had to seize my freedom. No matter what the cost, I had to win my independence. I made my plans.

A high rise block of apartments had been built at Highgate Hill, virtually around the corner from my father's house. I checked it out. The security was good. If you were a visitor you could gain entry only if the resident you wanted to see buzzed you in.

A two-bedroom apartment was available on the 10th floor. I took a one-year lease on it and installed a tenant (a total stranger who replied to an advertisement. She became a good friend and we keep in touch to this day).

I intended to move in as well but I was too frightened. A week went by, then another and another. I still could not pluck up the courage to move out of my father's house. My brother-in-law Gerardo knew of my misery. Being a Sicilian, albeit a liberated one, he understood my plight. He promised he would support me in my decision to strike out on my own.

I was 26, yet I still could not move. Because of my Sicilian conditioning, I believed the act of leaving home would be a terrible betrayal of my duty as a daughter. Leaving without the permission and blessing of my father was like breaking the law.

An almost hysterical war was going on in my mind, fuelled by a mixture of guilt over my intentions, despair over my situation and fear of the unknown forces I would unleash. In my imagination I devised the worst possible consequences.

They sound ridiculous and unreal as I think about them now, but in my mind, in the state it was in then, they were real possibilities.

But I was prepared for anything. Whatever the consequences were, I thought I'd much rather suffer it now than live this life of strictness, and endure these feelings of imprisonment.

Even though I was an adult, a 26-year-old woman, I was still answerable to my parents.

It sounds really funny as I share it, but it is true. I was prepared to go to any lengths to gain total independence.

I had heard of other Sicilian girls who had taken poison, the pesticide DDT. Like me, they used to work in vineyard blocks. You would hear that 17-year-old Theresa had just committed suicide. And I knew exactly what was happening because I was feeling the same way.

I remember the day I left as if it were yesterday.

It was a weekend in August 1977 and Elvis Presley had just died. My father had asked me to go picking grapes, so I went to the farm and did the picking of the grapes and the packing on the Saturday. On the Sunday I had to bottle the wine, another job of mine, which I did at home.

After I finished bottling the wine, he went off to the farm with my mother. My friend Marie Gillette was with me, so I said with more conviction than I really felt, 'Dad's left. Let's go'.

None of my other Australian girlfriends really understood my plight except Marie, who had enormous empathy. She did the packing. I was too stressed. I was a mess. I don't think I would ever have got out of that house without her help. I felt that my heart was breaking. Tears were streaming down my face as I wrote them a note with a shaking hand. It said:

```
Dear Mum and Dad,

I love you. If ever you are sick or need me I
will be with you. I have packed my bags and I
am now leaving home.

Love,

Sarina.
```

Marie guided me, sobbing, out of the house. I was shutting one door and opening another on a new chapter in my life. Little did I know that another drama was waiting for me around the corner.

I was about to learn that life can kick you in the face at a time when you are least prepared to deal with it.

The Lessons

These are the key lessons I would like you to take from what I have written in Chapter One:

1. The best form of revenge is massive success.

2. Whenever you have a problem, don't be too proud to ask for help. There will always be someone there to give you that help.

3. Don't blindly follow your conditioning. (I had been conditioned to believe that marriage was more important than a career, but I took the career option instead. And look where it got me!)

4. Education is the key to your future.

5. Never go backwards.

6. Find the right time – and the courage – to seize your freedom and independence

CHAPTER TWO

My desperate pursuit of independence

When I moved into my rental apartment I had dry ice in the bathroom because I couldn't afford a fridge. I slept on a single mattress on the floor, because I couldn't afford a bed. I used to take branches from trees and put them into champagne bottles because I couldn't afford plants.

I had my job as a legal secretary and as a night school typing teacher. I took on two other jobs – secretary to the body corporate of my apartment block and a job cleaning display units.

Having no savings, I was living from pay packet to pay packet. I made a decision. I would never be this financially desperate again because I didn't like that feeling

I had broken all contact with my family, except for my brother-in-law Gerardo who had helped give me the courage to strike out and make a life of my own. He had seen something in me that no-one else had.

He is a shrewd judge of character and an extremely level-headed man, kind, considerate, a good listener – and a wonderful husband to my sister. To this day I rely on his judgment over so many things.

He was the one I trusted at this time because I knew he was the only member of my family who would not put pressure on me to go back to my parents, or use emotional blackmail to make me reverse my decision.

Through him I learned what had happened when my mother and father returned home to discover my absence and find my note.

My father went into shock. It was as if the note had said his daughter had died. He behaved as if he were in mourning. My mother could only nibble at food and lost weight. My sisters, Rita and Rosina and my brother Joe, flew into rages because of my departure.

It was bad, but not as bad as I had feared. A month after leaving home, I plucked up the courage to go back and visit my mother and father.

Such emotion. They embraced me as if I were the prodigal daughter. My father pleaded with me to come back home, promising that I could have the freedom to do as I wished. We all cried.

My mother plied me with food as only Italian mothers can. But I stood firm. I told them I loved them both very dearly, but that I needed to have my freedom.

I discovered from this visit that I had not really understood my father at all. I had been blinded by the authoritarian figure, the tyrant whose word could not be challenged. This day I discovered that beneath that fearsome exterior, there was a father who loved his daughter dearly, a father who would never do anything in the world to hurt her.

He had honoured me by making me his apprentice – or more correctly, his lieutenant – and I know today that I have his influence to thank for my basic business skills. My father was an honourable man. He used to say to me, '*Sarina, you must always be honest, always tell the truth*' – and that is the code I live by: always tell the truth. Empower people with the truth.

Working those four jobs, I saved hard through my first year out on my own.

It sounds a lot, but after years of working for my father, four jobs were a breeze. Now I had most of the weekends free except for some cleaning duties, which were nothing compared with the weekend hard labour I was used to out on the vineyard.

Believe me, I had plenty of energy left over to go out on dates on Saturday nights and Sundays. I had a wonderful time.

I met and fell in love with young men who were successful and stimulating. I discovered the delights of dining at the finest restaurants, socialising with high achievers and driving fast cars. I was passionately happy. I was flying high!

There were irritations, of course. Some boy friends got serious about wanting to change me, telling me how to dress, how to speak, how to behave. I resisted. I moved on. I didn't want to be anyone else. I wanted to be me.

Most of all I didn't want to be anyone else's possession. I had not escaped from the restrictions and disciplines of my father's household only to lose my freedom to another man.

At the end of my first year out on my own, the apartments in my apartment block came onto the market. The developer was in financial difficulty and was going into liquidation.

Like many other tenants in the building, I saw an opportunity to buy my apartment at a favourable price. The developers needed the money didn't they? – and they needed it fast.

We could all see that. The real estate agency handling the sales was rushed by all the other tenants. I didn't go near the agents. Instead, I went straight to the accounting firm handling the liquidation and made an offer.

The accountant I met, Michael Wayland, was quite taken by this 27-year-old Italian girl who confronted him. And I didn't give him a chance. I poured on the charm and pointed out how much he would be saving in agent's commissions by making a direct sale. He was later to become my external accountant for five years after I began my commercial typing school business.

My strategy saved me $2500 off the purchase price, a lot of money for me at the time. In fact it was the difference between being able, or not being able, to make the purchase. I had gone to the National Bank for a loan and was staggered when they told me they didn't lend money to single women. I went to an insurance company, the SGIO and they agreed to lend me $35,000 over 30 years on the condition that it be a loan jointly to me and my mother, who without telling Dad, loaned me $2000 of her own money toward the purchase price.

I loved that apartment. It was brand new when I moved into it and it had such lovely views. I was so happy there.

But how things can change. Twelve months after buying it, I was fired from my legal secretary day job and my typing teaching job at night. I still had the mortgage and turning to my father was not an option because I sensed he would agree to help only on the condition that I return home.

I was really in a fix – but I was also in a rage because of what had happened. I turned that rage into a positive force. It was the rage that gave me the strength to change my life forever.

What happened was this: First, I was fired from my night job of teaching typing. When I took this class on, it had only a handful of students. Under me, it quickly grew to a capacity enrolment, a full house of paying students.

I was popular because I made the lessons fun. I had the class jumping out of their skins to music and laughing at my stories about my life. I had a motivational streak in me even then. I would tell them things like, *'never let anyone else tell you that you can't do it – you can be whatever you want to be. Look at me. A dream job is waiting for you, too'*.

I would constantly challenge them to keep thinking about how they were going to get that job and give them tips on how to go about it. They could tell I had a genuine interest in where they were going in their lives – and it was true, I really did.

So as word about me spread, more students applied to join the class.

But then I was fired. Why? Because my supervisor resented me. For some reason unknown to me, she had the idea I was dating her boyfriend. How wrong that was. But on that silly suspicion I was fired over the phone and without an exit interview.

Big mistake. The students were upset by my instant dismissal. They would not accept another teacher. They said they would stay away unless I was re-instated. So, to my complete surprise, I was asked to return. I did.

I had won that little war, but I was about to lose another.

Several weeks later, my legal boss fired me. There had been a 'situation' in the office involving him and his former secretary. The guy's wife suspected something and was putting him under a lot of pressure. So he fired me. Why? I've never been able to it work out. I guess it was the emotional turmoil he was going through.

His pretext was that I was five minutes late returning from lunch. He had warned me the day before that if I was late one more time I would be fired. I had been late a few times, but I had also worked many extra hours without overtime.

At lunch I lingered over a scalding hot cappuccino and I was a few minutes late back at the office as a result. He met me at the door and told me to go into his office, where he presented me with a cheque and told me I was finished.

I said: 'What about all of the weekends and nights I have worked here for eight months without any overtime?' But he was unmoved.

The bastardry of it had me absolutely incensed. I told him he would never have a peaceful night's sleep ever again because of what he was doing to me.

I was in real trouble. I wasn't earning enough at the night school to live on and pay off my mortgage. I had savings of $2600. I was crying as I went down the lift and out of the building to go home to my apartment.

When I entered the apartment I was hysterical. I cried and cried and screamed out in my loudest voice, *'I'll do it, or die'.*

What I meant by that was that I had to do something with my life. I had to move forward.

But how? ... and to what?

There was a half-formed idea in my head. I had been dating a barrister who was divorced from a woman who had established a commercial training school. He kept saying to me that his ex-wife, who was approximately 10 years older than me, had started up a school and why didn't I do the same?

I hadn't taken him seriously, but now I thought, why not?

I told my second flat mate what I was thinking of doing. She said, 'Don't do it. You can hardly express yourself in English'.

Everyone I spoke to told me, *'don't do it ... the high rent, the economy, the government, the failure rate of small businesses'.*

I was naive. The words 'don't' and 'can't' make me defiant. I went looking for a place to start a typing school and found a three-storey building in

The Golden Square in Albert Street, Brisbane that had a vacant room. The ground floor was a bank branch office, the second floor was occupied with a couple of small businesses and the top floor had this room that had been vacant for two years and it was terrible ... bare floors, peeling paint, exposed water pipes and ducting hanging beneath the ceiling. But it was cheap – $100 per week. And I had a vision. I could see a class in here, I could hear the rat-tat-tat of typewriters.

I could hear music, I could see bright young faces and I could see freedom and options for myself.

I also had a problem. I had little money. Only $2600. This place needed work on it. What about equipment? What about desks? What about staff?

I went to my father. I said, 'Dad, will you lend me some money to get started?'.

He said, 'Sarina I will not give you money for such a business. Go back and be a legal secretary again'.

I used $600 of my savings to pay for the formalities of forming a business and buying paint. I had $2000 left as working capital. I knew it would not be enough. How could such a small amount cover running costs and equipment like typewriters and word processors, furniture, staff and rent?

I went to my bank, Westpac, in which I now had that credit balance of $2000 and pitched my story. I told the bank manager about my success as a typing teacher and outlined my plan to open up a school that I would call 'The Office' Business Academy and it would teach typing, short-hand, book-keeping, English and word processing.

I spoke with more confidence and enthusiasm than I was really feeling inside, but at heart I am a sales person and right then I was in the business of selling myself to this bank manager. I had to sound good. I had to look good. I had to display outward certainty even though, inwardly, I was truly uncertain.

I looked him right in the eye. I smiled with my mouth. I smiled with my eyes. I modulated my voice to its most mellow tones.

And it worked! He agreed to loan me $3000 against the security of the $2000 I had remaining in my account. In effect, he was lending me just $1000.

I asked my brother in-law Ricardo, husband of my sister Rosina, to come to the building with me. Showing him the floor I had rented and the room which was to be the classroom, I said, 'Ricardo, would you paint this for me?'.

He shook his head in dismay, but then he said: 'Of course Sarina, I will help you. What colour would you like me to paint it?'.

I said, 'I would like you to paint the ceiling and the pipes chocolate brown'.

He said, 'Sarina, that is not a colour for ceilings. Ceilings should be light'.

I said, 'trust me. It will look great'.

I went to my brother Joe, a carpenter, and asked him: 'Joe, will you build me some desks?'.

'Sarina,' he said, 'perhaps one desk'.

'But I need more. I need at least 10 long desks,' I replied.

'I will build you one desk,' he insisted.

I begged, I pleaded, but he was unmovable. Finally, I burst into tears. He is a soft-hearted, kind man, my brother.

'Don't cry, Sarina,' he said. 'I'll build you two desks'.

I cried even harder.

'Come on, Sarina, stop that crying,' he said. 'I'll build you three.'

He had no hope. My tears were programmed for 10 desks. And when I finally dried my eyes and hugged him, 10 it was.

Life is beautiful. This was the brother who had verbally threatened to drag me back home after I had left and now he was helping me fulfil a dream. As today I am helping him fulfil his dream.

While all this work was going on I was out selling my 4-week courses at $333 per person. I was opening up dreams of opportunity for young women as secretary/receptionists to travel consultants, barristers and solicitors, doctors and dentists, hotels and motels, real estate agents, accountants and as executive secretaries in large and small organisations.

I had a brand new receipt book to write out receipts for the deposits the enrolees were paying me. When I signed up my first student, I didn't give her the receipt numbered one in the book. I gave her receipt No. 10. I didn't want her to think she was my first student.

I promised my prospective students that as well as training in job skills I would have real doctors, lawyers, dentists, bank officers, corporate executives and public relations experts coming into their classroom to lecture them on in-office situations and procedures. I was able to make that promise because I had done the rounds of the professions in the city and arranged it with qualified people in those fields.

I was proud to say in the enrolment brochure I produced: *'Be stimulated by the friendly and warm atmosphere of 'The Office' where you can feel secure in knowing that your training is the first step toward a rewarding, well-paid and professional career'.*

I made a promise that was to be a key force in the growth of my business over the ensuing rears: *Special training is given for that all-important first interview and on completion of the course our efficient job placement service is available to you free'.*

I told my students that as well as their specific skills courses, I would give them lessons in personality and confidence development, I would put them through invigorating programs on how to look and how to make beauty fun, advice on what to look for when they were buying or planning a wardrobe, instruction in speaking up, saying it properly and saying it at the right time, and in understanding exactly what their career position entailed.

I had set September 10, 1979 as the opening date of my academy, but when that date arrived I had sold only three courses. Not enough. It wasn't a good omen. I had to postpone the opening. I set a new date: September 17 and went to work to recruit more students. I signed up another seven. So that was 10 four-week courses at $333, paid in advance, adding $3330 to my working capital.

On the first day, one of the 10 decided not to continue. She walked out and went to Key Personnel. Ironically, Key Personnel later went out of business and I'm still going.

I was so upset about losing that student that I lost my voice for a few days. I made it up to my remaining students by extending their course by a week to ensure they received extra training value and a job of their choice. And it worked.

I called my school 'The Office' Business Academy because I thought it was a really cool name. Students could say, *I'm going back to the office.*

I decided I couldn't call it after me, firstly because I had been fired so many times and nobody would have wanted to pursue a fired legal secretary. Secondly, I loved the name more than my own name, I hired a part-time commercial teacher to teach shorthand, book-keeping and English. I would take the typing and word processing classes and I hired a part-time junior to assist us both. And I had that team of professionals coming in to lecture the students on what was involved in working in their businesses.

Memories of that first day in September 1979 are indelibly imprinted on my mind. We had just 10 desks, chocolate-coloured ceilings and pipes and a grass mat covering the floorboards in the classroom. My father had insisted on helping Ricardo with the painting, his way of saying he was with me in spirit, even though he would not lend me any money.

Let me digress here. When I was about to begin writing this book, I dined with my co-author in a Melbourne restaurant called Langton's. It is one of Melbourne's trendiest, patronised by the smart set. It is in a basement.

As I sat at my table, I looked up. What did I see? The ceiling was concrete and hanging from it were pipes and ducts. And they were all painted chocolate brown – ceilings, pipes, ducts, the lot. What a fantastic coincidence.

I pointed it out to my co-author. He said, 'I've been in here many times, and I've never noticed the ceiling. But now that you point it out I think it looks great'.

I smiled to myself and thought: *you didn't notice the ceilings because the chocolate brown softened them and allowed your focus to be drawn to what is really important about this place: the ambience, the lovely white table cloths, the cutlery, the glassware, the people.*

Before the renovations, my first classroom was rough and ready. Yes. But I was going to take the focus off that ugly ceiling by charging the room with passion. I was going to weave dreams of success with the young people who would be my students.

I was excited and terrified at the same time and suffered nights of insomnia walking around my apartment thinking, *what am I doing?*

What was I letting myself in for? What if I could not sign up enough students to get sufficient cash flow going to cover the rent, the wages of the part-time senior teacher and the part-time junior I had engaged and the mortgage on my apartment?

If only I had known I was about to get a tap on the shoulder by the friendly finger of destiny.

The Lessons

These are the key lessons I would like you to take from what I have written in Chapter Two:

1. Always be honest and tell the truth. This will empower you and others.

2. Don't be afraid to go straight to the source. (I did and it saved me a lot of money in a property purchase.)

3. Never let anyone tell you that you can't do it – strive to be whatever you want to be.

4. Don't be put off by pessimists: *'Don't do it ...the high rent, the economy, the government, the failure rate'.*

5. Have a vision.

CHAPTER THREE

The words that inspired me

About six months after opening my school, I bought a ticket to attend a seminar being conducted by a motivational speaker from the US. The speaker's name was Jim Rohn.

Listening to Jim Rohn that night 22 years ago, I learned a lesson that has stayed with me ever since, a lesson that continues to inspire me, and is still my guiding light.

Jim Rohn told a story about a friend of his, a successful man who had a stock answer when anyone asked him what they needed to do to earn an above-average income. The answer was: '*Become an above-average person. Work on yourself. Develop an above average-handshake. Develop an above-average smile. Develop above-average skills, above-average passion, an above-average walk -- walk as if you were an apprentice millionaire.*'

And then in telling that story Jim Rohn spoke the words I believe can unlock the door to success for anyone. '***To have more, become more. Work harder on yourself than on your job. The major key to your better future is you.***'

The essence of his message was that two people can be selling the same product, but one sells more than the other. Why? Because one has the magic and one does not.

The magic is not in the product. It's inside the individual. The passion, the enthusiasm, puts a power into the handshake. It puts conviction into your case. And it attracts positive energy because you have an above average attitude and a strong belief in yourself.

Oh it was such heady stuff, and it couldn't have reached my ears at a better time in my life.

You are the difference. Yes, yes! Make yourself the difference. Yes, yes, yes!

It wasn't long before more students were signing up. It wasn't only through advertising. Just as much, it was through existing students telling their family and friends.

I had worked out that to help people, you had to make it fun. You had to believe in them. You had to care for them. You had to go the extra mile. You had to help them find a job that would lead them to their dream job.

No matter how great the training you gave, your students would not feel fulfilled and satisfied until you could help them get that job. And you had not really achieved anything until they got that job. That was the principle that drove the growth of my education, training and employment business.

I knew how to go out and get that job because I had done it so many times.

I had, and still do have, a lot of empathy with people who were in my situation with no money, no training, no job. I really could relate to them all.

So I made our classes fun. I started giving motivational lectures daily, drawn from the philosophies and concepts I had learned from Jim Rohn, Denis Waitley and others.

I developed an individual rapport with every single student. One on one. Me, provoking, joking, challenging each student to do more today than they did yesterday, last week, last year. I would say to them, 'I will always tell you the truth. I expect you to do the same for me.'

Students would share their fears and dreams with me and I would listen and support them in every way possible to realise their full potential and their vision. Through this process I was beginning what was to become my life's work. I knew then that if they did not succeed in getting satisfactory jobs, I had not succeeded. Their success was my success. That was the win-win culture I was determined to create and did create. If you win, I win. If you fail, I fail. Powerful words.

I would tell the new teachers who joined us as our enrolment grew: 'People see us as a place to teach business skills, but we're really much more than that. We have to be passionate about enhancing people's lives.

'Yes, we will improve their chances of getting a job by developing or refreshing their job skills, but I want us to offer a lot more. I want to give them confidence to go out and get that job. I want us to develop them personally so that they can go into a better job knowing they will perform and live a passionate and fulfilled life.'

I personally involved myself in their job searches. Each of my students knew that they were important to me and I to them. They knew how determined I was for them to succeed and they responded with matching determination.

It was my custom to have assemblies every morning. I would ask each student what he or she was doing about getting a job, how many visits were they making to the CES (Commonwealth Employment Service) to find a job? I told them going to the CES was like going to pray in church – it was kind of mandatory.

And they had to inform me. I was just driven. With me around, they had no choice once they came in. I would tell them how good they were, how special they were and how much they deserved to succeed. There was only one way up!

I made them realise their future was just as important to me as it was to them. I made them believe they mattered. It's great to believe that you matter. You care more about yourself then. And you try harder to be better. And they all did.

For me, it was a passion. The first person I got a job for was a bank manager's wife who hadn't worked for about 15 years. She signed up for a four-week refresher course in typing and secretarial skills.

Everyone told me it was impossible to retrain someone in four weeks and give them enough confidence and skills to be able to go out and get a job.

But with her commitment, and the passion of my support, she did. I called my brother-in-law Gerardo and asked him to ask around. As a solicitor in general practice he knew a lot of professionals in the city.

Besides, he was a director of the company I had set up to run my business. I needed someone in my life at that time to be a solid, common sense sounding board with some knowledge of business. Gerardo was the ideal person to be my co-director and fill that role.

He called a friend of his, a chartered accountant, who said he would take her on. She took the job and held it for 15 years of her working life.

That's the way it went. In our early days, I would cajole all my friends and contacts to give my people jobs. Later, as the word spread in the business community that our graduates were confident, positive people, as well as having good skills, it became easy to place them in jobs.

I started getting calls from big businesses that had taken one or more of our graduates, asking if I could send them more like the ones they had already employed.

When I opened the school, I told myself, I'm going to give myself six months and if it doesn't work, I can always go back to a legal job. Always. I knew that. I was good at getting fired but I was also very good at job interviews and winning jobs.

But after six weeks, I knew it was going to work. And there I was, for the first time in my life, enjoying freedom and happiness. I had found a job that was really not a job, but a game of life.

I made more money in the first three months than I did as a Legal Secretary in a year.

I was doing really well. I was on fire in every sense.

Do you think I was excited? I was really happy. I was there. I was the apprentice today, but a future millionaire. I was the apprentice clerk or painter, the apprentice teacher, the apprentice of everything. I just did the lot. I worked 15 hours a day seven days a week for the first two years. I didn't stop. I was just so excited.

There was one problem. To achieve the real growth I was seeking, to have any real future in this business, I had to win government accreditation for the courses I was offering.

Without that accreditation, I couldn't continue to grow and get the recognition a training college needed to have.

When I approached the government to ask for my courses to be accredited, the bureaucrats I spoke to said they would never ever dream of it because my courses were too short.

One of them told me 'you will never get it (accreditation).'

I hung in there, making appointment after appointment to see the officer-in-charge. He kept saying 'no', and as more and more of my students succeeded (I was achieving a 98 per cent success rate in getting them jobs) I said to this man: 'Think of a delicious cake.

I have all the ingredients. Look at what I'm doing. My courses may be different, but you know they're the best. We do get people jobs. You must give me accreditation. We'll show the department that my ingredients really work'.

I never gave up. It took months, but finally we got it approved.

A colleague of mine asked one of the executives, who was involved in the decision to grant me accreditation, what he thought of my persistence. The executive made these generous remarks: 'Sarina was the most determined person I had ever met. Whatever a person needs to succeed, she had it. She had the aura of someone who was destined to succeed'.

Another lesson there: Persistence pays.

Government approval gave me the status I needed and I used it in my advertising. I was now getting a flow of enrolments. My business made more money in the first month after accreditation than it had in the first six months of its existence.

I needed more space for my students. There was a guy called Andy George who, on my request, gave up his office for my expansion and he moved to the lower level. There was another man who had been in the building for 30 years. He used to manufacture soap for dermatitis. I said to him, 'I would like to expand into your area'.

He said, 'never, never'. But he finally decided to retire and we moved into his space. Within two years we occupied all of the third floor and part of the second. We were booming. We were a success and people were talking.

It was a wonderful, exhilarating time in my life. Everything was going right. I went from driving a Toyota Celica to an RX7 sports car.

I'd drive by a plate glass window and look at me sitting in the driver's seat of that racy RX7. I thought I was gorgeous and had a destination.

I bought myself a holiday apartment on the beachfront at Surfers Paradise. It's an Italian tradition. Whenever you can, buy property. It's better than money in the bank.

With memories of how I used dry ice in the bath in place of a refrigerator when I first bought my Brisbane apartment, I decided I had to have an American refrigerator with an ice-making facility in the new holiday apartment.

Everything was going so well, I treated my father to an overseas trip to Italy. Jokingly, I said to him, 'Dad, I just want to thank you for being so mean, for not giving me even $100 to help me start my business'.

I really did feel I owed him something. He passed on to me the ethic of hard work and it was from him I inherited the street smarts that mean so much in dealing with people.

I said, 'I just want you to go to Italy and have a great time'.

He went to Sicily, to Castiglione, and told the relatives I was too busy to get married.

And then disaster struck. The building caught fire. We were lucky to get out with our lives. In fact, some of us were trapped on the third floor in thick smoke and I was getting ready to jump when a senior teacher arrived and slapped me across the face to stop me.

The fire brigade put the fire out in the lower basement before major damage was done.

Luckily it was at the end of the year and we were due to break up for Christmas. It had been such a good year in all other respects that I decided to take a holiday overseas while the building was being repaired.

Fortunately, the fire had been confined, so structural damage was minimal. Smoke damage was the biggest worry in my area.

I didn't expect there would be any problems in getting the building back to shape, but I was to come back from my holiday to some shocking news. The bank that owned the building had given us notice to quit the premises because of safety concerns.

No building. No school. This was my life! What was I to do now?

Look for a silver lining, that's what. And I found it. You always do when you look hard enough, with the right attitude.

The start of a new life. A shipboard photo of Sarina, 5, standing at her mother Maria's knee during their voyage from Sicily to Australia in 1956 to join Sarina's father Antonino in Brisbane, Australia. Her sister Rosina is second from left and her other sister Rita is second from right.

Sarina returns to Castiglione the Sicilian town of her birth, in 2001 for the first time in 18 years.

Antonino Russo at work on his vineyard at Wacol, Queensland.

Sarina and her father on her confirmation day.

Antonino Russo (lying down front left) in North Africa with the Italian Army in World War II.

Antonino Russo packs grapes on his Wacol vineyard.

*Sarina aged 10 with mother
Maria and father Antonino.*

*Antonino Russo, with wife Maria on his left, makes a speech at the
wedding of Sarina's sister Rosina to Ricardo Berlese.*

Sarina with her mother and father after starting her business 'The Office' Business Academy.

*Joe Russo and his wife Maria with their daughter Tina and
Tina's daughter Stephanie at a family celebration.*

Sarina and her father take a rest from work at the Wacol vineyard.

Sarina wins the Miss Italy award in a Brisbane beauty pageant in 1971. With her is brother-in-law Gerardo Pennisi.

Sarina's mother Maria celebrates her 89th birthday in October 2002. She is shown here between her son Joe and Joe's wife Maria. Behind them, grandson Michael Pennisi plays prankster with his cousin Maria Berlese.

Seven of Sarina's eight nephews at the wedding of Sarina's niece Angela Berlese to Louis Esposito at St Stephen's Cathedral in Brisbane. From left: Tony Russo, Gino Russo, John Berlese, Mark Berlese, Marcello Pennisi (with red bow tie) Andrew Pennisi and David Pennisi.

Sarina's brother Joe entertains with his squeeze box.

After moving her business into the MLC Tower building in Brisbane in 1983, Sarina lets her mother try her office chair on the 26th floor.

Sarina and members of her family with President Bill Clinton at the Brisbane dinner at which Sarina was hostess to the President. From left, her brother-in-law Gerardo Pennisi, his son Andrew, The President, Sarina and Mark Berlese. Front: Marcello Pennisi and David Pennisi, also sons of Gerardo.

In March 2002 the Sarina Russo Group presented an evening with President Bill Clinton in aid of the Royal Children's Hospital, Brisbane. Sarina and her nephew Marcello Pennisi are shown here at the function with Queensland Premier Peter Beattie who welcomed Bill Clinton to Brisbane.

Sarina (second from left) at lunch with Kevin Aye (General Manager of Sarina Russo Job Access), Debbie Auton (Manager, Seymour, Victoria, office of SRJA), Lorraine Nesbitt (Regional Operations Manager of SRJA, Victoria) and Dudley Martin a former SRJA senior executive.

Sarina with nephew Tony Russo (rear left), Ricardo Berlese (front left), David Pennisi and Michael Pennisi.

The Lessons

These are the key lessons I would like you to take from what I have written in Chapter Three:

1. Work on yourself to become an above-average person.

2. The major key to your future is you. To have more, become more.

3. If you win, I win. If you fail, I fail.

4. Persistence pays. It was only through persistence that I won government accreditation for the courses I was offering at my fledgling business academy. When I got it, my business rapidly expanded.

5. Whenever you can, buy property. It's better than money in the bank.

6. In times of adversity you'll always find a silver lining if you look hard enough, with a can-do attitude.

CHAPTER FOUR

Adversity strikes, opportunity beckons

I telephoned Gerardo during my Christmas break in Italy and asked how things were going. He told me there were no problems. He was protecting me. He knew that the bank had served us with a notice to vacate their building, but he didn't want to spoil my holiday, so he kept it from me until my return.

It was a nice thought, but when he told me on my arrival home, I was angry. He rode out my storm in his typical 'no-point-in-getting-upset' style. And, in truth, he had calculated it pretty well. There wasn't much I could have done, even if I had been here when the bank issued the notice to quit.

When I calmed down, I said to myself: this is not an unlucky break, it's an opportunity. My school can afford to be in a better building, in a better area of the city, anyway. Here's my chance to do something about that.

How could I have thought differently when one of my favourite pep talks to my students and staff would go like this: It's your attitude that makes the difference. Some people have an attitude that gets them into a state of mind of believing everything to be difficult in their lives. They keep complaining, *why does it always happen to me?* The answer is, it really happens to all of us. What you have to realise is, it's not so much what happens to you that matters, it's what you do about it that's important.

'You have the choice to look at the situation or event and change your attitude by not just seeing it as a negative, but to see it as an opportunity ... whether it is an opportunity to learn something about people, or to learn something about life, or to learn something about yourself'.

I felt entitled to give talks like that because of the many rejections and failures I have experienced in my life and it was precisely because of them, or how I reacted to them, that I got to where I am today.

I made some calls to real estate agents and learned there was space available for lease on the 26th floor of one of the city's choicest – and tallest – buildings, the MLC Centre.

I had recently read a book by Zig Ziglar, one of the world's great motivators. Its title was *See You At The Top* – a really inspiring book. Could this be an omen?

When I inspected the vacant space on the 26th floor, I felt with excitement that indeed it was an omen. Up here, we really were at the top. There was no taller building in the city at the time. The view was absolutely stunning.

I decided I had to have it, but almost choked when the agent told me how much the annual lease would cost. It was ten times more than what I had been paying in the bank building. I would be going from $5000 a year to $50,000.

This was a major test of my confidence in myself. I looked back to where I had come from, I thought about what I had achieved, I recalled all of the obstacles I had run into and climbed over and I thought of the book *See You At The Top,* and I said to myself *it can be done!*

The ironic thing was that my last job as a legal secretary had been in this same building. This was where I had been fired by the solicitor who got

CRISIS MANAGEMENT
"TURN ADVERSITY INTO EMPOWERMENT"

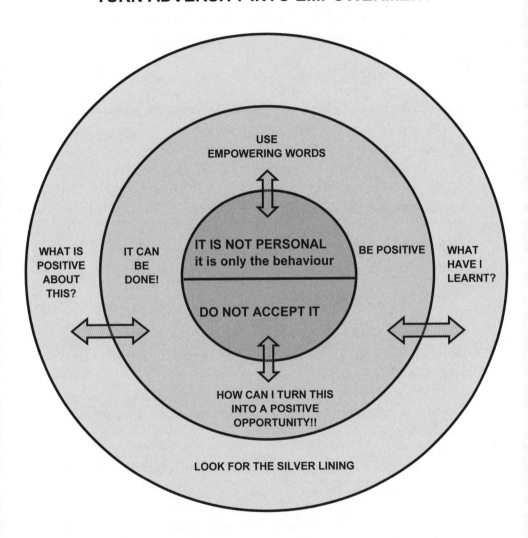

Remember :

"The pain of discipline weighs ounces; the pain of regret weighs tons"

his personal life into a tangle. When I was inspecting the building I ran into this solicitor who had personally sent me packing. He said, 'what are you doing up here?'.

I said, 'I'm starting a new business here. I had to leave the other building because they condemned it.'

'You'll never make it,' he said.

That was the first thing he said. He could have said, 'well, how are you?'. But the first thing he said, was, ' you'll never make it. The economy, the high rent'.

Because I was doing well, I said, 'what's wrong with the economy? I don't know anything about it. Is it bad? Or good?'.

He said, 'you'll never make it. The government, the recession, the taxes'.

So I had another night of insomnia ... that enormous jump from $5000 a year in rent to $50,000 a year was such a fearful leap.

I was walking around the floor hoping my flatmate would not see me, thinking, oh my God, what am I doing? Three years at $50,000 a year. How am I going to do it?

Gerardo, as my co-director, said to me, 'Sarina, this is a quantum leap. Can you manage it?'.

I ignored all of the warnings, signed a three-year lease and we moved in. *'See you at the top'* became our slogan ... and we grew and grew.

We had momentum. Our students and graduates spread the story about how much they enjoyed our courses and how easy they found it to get jobs on graduation – and how beautiful the environment was with air conditioning in the summer heat.

I was hosting a weekly television chat program on a major metropolitan TV network. It's still going today, after 18 years. My segment is entitled

How to Get That Job. My guests are people from all walks of life; employers, government spokespeople, representatives of the companies that recruit staff from our graduate ranks, and our own students and graduates.

Invariably the company representatives say they like to recruit our graduates because they are so enthusiastic and have such positive attitudes. Our students and graduates describe the great difference our courses made to their lives.

I speak about the value of living with passion and aiming for the top.

I talk about life being full of uncertainties, but I get the message across that there's one thing we must feel certain about and that's ourselves. We've got to feel good about ourselves.

My message is that if you haven't already started to do so, start now, start feeling good about yourself.

No matter what other people think about you, it doesn't matter. You can just say to them, 'I'll consider it for the next 30 seconds'.

Unless you think you're No. 1, unless you believe you're great, unless you believe you have the potential to do more, nobody else is going to really believe in you. So it's important that you start within.

Become intelligently selfish about who it is you want to be and start doing it today. If you can, you can then share more. If you're happy, you can share happiness. If you're depressed, what will you share?... depressed feelings? Do people want to be around depressed people? No.

It's very important that you start within yourself and feel good about yourself. Start looking at what it is that you'd like to change. One of the things I say is, *accept who you are today, in pursuit of what you want to be tomorrow.*

I close each TV segment with words like ... '*ciao for now. I'll see you at the top*'.

In those early shows – and also today – I was holding out hopes and dreams to the young people of the city of Brisbane and the State of Queensland and they responded to my message, both by enrolling in our courses and winning good jobs after their graduation.

We aligned ourselves to the needs of the business community, fine-tuning or expanding our courses to fit the career opportunities that were opening up under the advance of technology.

I was on such a high as the business continued to grow that I decided I wanted a Mercedes convertible. I went to the bank and said I would like to purchase a new Mercedes for approximately $72,000. That was in 1985. You could then buy a four-bedroom house for that much on a large block of land within four kilometres of the Brisbane city centre.

The bank manager looked at me as if I was out of my mind and said, '*Christ, you could buy a house with that much*'. Then he proceeded to give me a long lecture about tying up so much money in an asset of such diminishing value.

I was angry at his patronizing, killjoy manner. I got up, told him I didn't want his 'dirty money' and slammed the door as I walked out. I checked with my accountant and he said, 'you can do this in your own right within the next six months'.

That's exactly what I did. I bought one. I just looked so good driving past a plate glass window.

Two years after moving into the MLC Centre my father became seriously ill with adult onset diabetes. A week after being admitted to hospital he had a stroke and died. For me, for my mother and my brother and my sisters - and for all our extended family - it seemed as if the world had come to stop. We were inconsolable in our grief. We just could not believe that he had gone. We all thought he was immortal. He was the indestructible one, so strong, so certain, so protective. So fiercely proud of his strength. He was our patriarch. He was so revered by the Italian community that St Brigid's Church at Red Hill where we had worshipped as a family every Sunday was overflowing with mourners at his funeral service. The priest who conducted the service said that the attendance was bigger than the Christmas Sunday congregation.

My Dad was beloved in the Italian community because he was always there to lend a hand to anyone in trouble. They said about him 'he would give you the shirt off his back'. And he really would. He was that kind of man. He also had many Australian friends who attended his funeral.

We commissioned an architect to design a marble chapel which we had built at Mt Gravatt cemetery and we laid him to rest there. Inside there is an altar. As a family we often recall stories of how he had exercised his strength and imposed his iron will.

It was really hard to carry on after he died. For two years I would burst into tears whenever I thought of him, which was often. Even today memories of him can bring tears to my eyes.

I escaped my grief by throwing myself into my business with even greater urgency and passion.

It seemed the growth in demand for our services would never stop.

There were other businesses on the 26th floor. There was one called Short Term Acceptance. I used to walk past it and say, 'short term it is'. And it was. It was not long before we took over their space.

There was another one, a computer company. It went broke and we took the area it was in. A Building Society occupied another corner.

I said to the manager, 'I need your corner. Would you re-allocate?'.

'Over my dead body,' he said.

A month later he was dead. I was in Hong Kong on business when I got a message to say he had died and his space was available. I felt terrible. The poor man had cancer.

I felt a bit shaky when we moved into his space. I was imagining ghosts. I made sure my own office was not in his corner.

I had set a goal that I was going to turn over $1 million. It took me about five years to turn over my first $1 million and by then I had taken over the whole of the 26th floor and part of the floor below that.

I heard that the solicitor who had fired me was reducing. I called him in and said, 'we can help you. We'll take over some of your floor space'.

He said, 'I beg your pardon?'.

I said, 'we'd love to'.

So he sub-leased some of his office space to us.

When I sent him cheques to pay for our sub-lease, it was the first time I ever got excited about paying my bills. I would attach a "with compliments" slip and I'd write on it: 'With excitement I enclose herewith $2000'.

What a feeling. This man had fired me, and now I was helping him with his rent. I just love that feeling. *The best form of revenge is massive success.* I felt good. I wanted to work harder and smarter.

In 1989, 10 years after I opened my typing school in one room over a bank, my business had grown to such an extent that I was invited to become a member of an organisation called the Young Presidents' Organisation (YPO). It was a great honour to be invited – and to be the first Queensland woman to have been invited – to join this select group. But most of all it was an incredible learning experience.

The YPO is a world-wide organisation, an economic and intellectual alliance of the CEOs of companies which together spin more than US$2 trillion in the global economy annually and employ more than 8 million people in more than 72 nations.

To be nominated for membership it is necessary to be below the age of 44 and to be the president, chairman, CEO, managing director or managing partner of a corporation or a division.

You must have at least 50 full-time employees under your control and you must meet dollar volume requirements based on the type of corporation you run, or your business must have an enterprise value of several million dollars.

Membership of this organisation opened up unimaginable new learning opportunities for me through seminars and international conferences it conducted for its members. These conferences are called 'universities' and they focus on specific topics such as mergers, acquisitions, international trade agreements and technology developments.

World leaders sometimes attend these 'universities' to give addresses and to answer questions. I have been exposed to the thinking of many great minds.

The YPO has alliances with the Harvard Business School, which offers intense, cutting-edge business education tailored exclusively for YPO members.

I saw these courses as a fantastic opportunity to advance my learning. I eagerly signed up for my first course in 1992. I loved it so much that I committed myself to continue attending.

So once a year, for the past 10 years, I have been going back to the Harvard Business School, studying alongside other YPO members, under the world's most eminent business educators.

Each year we take case studies of real companies and analyse them in teams under group leaders who are high achievers as business leaders. During our examination of these businesses, we talk about our own experiences and what we would do if we were the CEO of the company we were studying.

Self education is an investment in your future and the courses I was taking were expensive. Returning from my first visit to Harvard, I put myself through the cost versus value argument. On the one hand it seemed that what I was paying for a single week was a huge indulgence. On the other hand, what I had learned in a single week, not only from the course, but from the YPO members who were studying with me, had given me a totally new perspective about business. I felt stronger and more confident.

After returning to Harvard four times it was suggested that I do the Owner President Management Course, which is equivalent to an MBA. It involved three annual visits of three weeks at a time for extremely intensive study and examinations.

The cost was more than twice as much as for the single week courses I had been attending. I said to myself, this is a lot of money to spend on myself. Maybe I should settle for the annual weekly courses.

I had buddied up with another YPO member, Lucille Roberts, who was the CEO of a New York company many times bigger than mine. She said to me: 'Sarina, do it. Once you graduate out of this course, you will take your company to another level'. Her prediction turned out to be true.

We were in the MLC building for 11 years. I would come back from Harvard each year with fresh energy and greater determination to keep growing. I was opening up even greater opportunities for the other side of my business; recruitment and job placement.

With me, employment always went with training. There was no way that any of my students were not going to get jobs.

I used to take pride in saying that 99 per cent of my students got jobs. No-one ever left my courses without me seeing them and doing an exit interview.

If they needed extra training I'd give them extra, and if I needed to increase my numbers because I thought the class was looking small, I used to let them stay there at my cost, because it's all about atmosphere of learning, looking busy and feeling important with other inspiring students.

One day one of my accountants said to me: 'Sarina, you are paying so much out in rent, you should buy your own building'.

I said, 'I love it here. I love the view. The students are here because they like being on the 26th floor of the smartest building in the city'.

He said, 'no, Sarina, when you are looking out from your own building, that is the best view you can have'.

With those words, I was convinced. I made a phone call to first one, then a number of agents and told them what I wanted: a building in the Central Business District with so many floors, so much space.

No-one phoned me back. I should have known. They weren't taking me seriously. A woman buying prime CBD real estate in the 1990s? Not likely. We are talking millions of dollars here. What woman could afford that?

I got tired of waiting for a call-back, so I rang Gerardo and said, 'I'm not getting a response from these real estate agents. Don't they believe I'm serious about buying a city building?'.

He said, 'obviously not, Sarina. I'll see what I can do'.

Then an agent named John Dwyer called me and said, 'I've got a building to show you'.

He took me to a 12-storey building in Ann Street. I said, 'sorry John, I think I've given you the wrong brief. I wasn't expecting a high rise. I was thinking, maybe two, three floors'.

He said, 'no, come up to the top'. So we went straight to the rooftop where there is a terrace with a stunning view. He said: 'what do you think of this?'.

I was already visualizing what I could do up here – barbecues, office parties to celebrate a success or a milestone or just an inspiring spot to retreat to and think.

I said, 'it's magnificent. I like it'.

He said, 'would you like to buy it?'.

'I'd love to buy it,' I replied. 'It would be great.'

I called Gerardo, my common sense co-director and conservative commercial lawyer, told him about the building and asked him what he thought.

'I don't know about this,' he said. 'Do you think we have enough money?'.

We were in a healthy cash position, but we didn't have enough to cover the full cost. I said, 'Let's try the banks for the balance'.

I was optimistic but my optimism was ill-founded. I had overlooked an important reality. I thought of myself as a successful business person. I should have remembered that I was a woman.

A woman asking for a loan of a more than a million dollars to buy a high-rise building in the heart of the city? You've got to be joking.

My own bank said they would loan me the balance but would not lend me the extra $250,000 I knew I would need to renovate the ground floor to be the showcase of our company.

I went to the National Australia Bank where I was interviewed by a manager named Paul Anderson.

I had been putting a lot of student loans through his bank and when I said to him, 'I need a loan', he replied: 'Not a problem. Are you ready to answer 55 questions?'.

I said, 'yes'. He gave me a list of the questions and I went back to the office and typed out answers to the whole 55. If it was a test, I passed, because he gave me the loan.

Why did he say yes and the others say no? Because he looked not at my assets, but at the business and my ability. I would have thought that after 13 years of success and continuous growth, the others would also have looked at my ability.

They didn't look past the value of my assets.

Imagine how much more I thought of Paul than the others. He was to get my business from then on.

My co-author asked him why he had decided to give me the loan. Paul replied: 'The truth is that whether she was a man or a woman was not an issue with me. I judged her on the viability of her business and how good she was as an individual. I formed the opinion that she had an extreme determination to succeed, with huge drive and energy.

'Through her answers to those 55 questions, she laid out her vision so clearly that I could see it and understand it. It was clear to me that it was time for her to take her business to the next level and that was what the new building was all about – taking it to the next level.

'I thought to myself, this is a woman on the trail of success. She is one of the sharpest business people I have met and her networking ability is the best I have ever seen.

'I remembered when she came to me to ask about the student loans. I had said to her that what she was really asking me to do was to provide her students with deferred loans, because they could only afford to pay the interest while they were studying. We would have to wait until they graduated and got jobs before they could pay the principal off.

'I said to her, "what if they don't get jobs?" and she looked at me and said: "All of my students get jobs. I make sure they do".

'So I took a risk on her then and she was as good as her word. All of her students got jobs. Not one defaulted on a loan. And if they lost their jobs she took them back into her academy and gave them more training at her own cost and sent them out to get new jobs.'

Paul's decision to back me was the biggest turning point in my life.

I have to confess that in buying that building, I was scared to death. I had never owned anything as big, or as costly, as that.

Cost is relative. You could purchase a book by a great motivator like Anthony Robbins, or a business book by Jack Welch, one of the great business leaders of the past 100 years, and it may cost you $35. And you could think that's a high price to pay for a book. But first think about the investment in knowledge and then think about the value.

In thinking through the pros and cons of buying that high-rise building, I equated value versus cost. Yes, the cost was going to stretch me. This would be the biggest purchase of my life, but what about the value to my business? This building would give it a major presence in the city. It would be a landmark.

In value terms it was an easy decision. I had to go for it.

All of a sudden I was a landlord.

My competitor thought I had just bought a floor.

I said, 'no, I loved it so much I bought the building'.

When we moved in, it was very exciting. I thought I should show it to my mother. (Dad had passed away.) I told her, 'Mum, I have bought a building that is going to make you feel so proud'.

She said, 'let's have a look at it'. So I drove her to the front of the building in my Mercedes.

I said, 'what do you think Mum?'.

She looked up and down the building and said: 'oh my God. Why don't you just go and find yourself a husband.' So I jokingly said: 'Mum, don't you think it will enhance my chances?'.

I had to immediately look at my products because I only needed three floors of the building.

But I didn't want any tenants, not after the struggle I had gone through in the MLC centre in taking over the space of other tenants.

Gerardo and I disagreed over that issue. The Medibank health insurance group, a blue chip client, wanted to lease the ground floor.

I said, 'no, if I give the ground floor to Medibank and I have to have my foyer on the first floor, my showcase is never going to be what I dream it to be'.

Gerardo said, 'you should keep Medibank They'll pay you a good rent.'

And I said, 'I will sell more courses as a result of having my showcase, the foyer and reception, on the ground floor.'

I had hundreds of thousands of dollars in renovation costs and most of it went on the ground floor. Even today it still looks great. I created an image and a branding. I created something unique and inviting for the world to see.

But when we first moved in, my entire operation occupied only three of the 12 usable floors. How was I going to fill the rest? That was my next challenge.

The Lessons

These are the key lessons I would like you to take from what I have written in Chapter Four:

1. Unlucky breaks can be lucky opportunities.

2. It's your attitude that makes the difference.

3. Embrace rejections and failures. How you react to them makes you what you are today.

4. In a world of uncertainty strive to feel certain about yourself.

5. Accept who you are today in pursuit of what you want to be tomorrow.

6. The best view you can have is from a building that is yours.

7. Find a banker who looks not just at your assets, but at you and what you have achieved.

CHAPTER FIVE

The biggest risk of my business life

Sometimes people fail to commit because they fear the worst. Such a fear could have stopped me buying the high rise building at 82 Ann Street because in making that purchase I was taking a real risk – and I knew it.

In buying that building, I was removing my business from a secure environment in which it was flourishing. I was leaving a beautiful building with great views, great facilities. It had been our home for 11 years, and it was synonymous with the slogan that had carried us to fame in the State of Queensland – *see you at the top!*

Leaving it was like changing your brand name from something universally known to something unknown.

Furthermore, the new building was secondary standard accommodation. Would the dynamics, the energy and the synergy that had been going on for several years in my previous headquarters work in a 12-storey building?

That was my risk. Why did I take it? Because I had developed a philosophy about risk. See the worst-case scenario of a deal, be clear in your mind about what the consequences of that worst-case scenario will be and be prepared to accept them, but never let fear cloud your judgement.

I said to myself, if I don't do this, if I don't follow through and make this building and my business a landmark in the city, I will always regret it. My advice to myself and others is never to regret anything in your life. The pain of discipline weighs ounces, the pain of regret weighs tons.

I knew I had to make a commitment. I named the building 'The Sarina Russo Centre'.

I had no false modesty about naming the building after myself. It was time to cash in on my public profile. There had been articles in newspapers and magazines for some years about the successes of Sarina Russo, the principal of 'The Office' Business Academy (now RIT), who worked by the slogans *how to get that job* and *see you at the top*.

Through those articles and my weekly television spot, the name Sarina Russo had become associated in the public mind with business and career training and finding jobs. It was time to cement the connection: think training and job-getting; *think Sarina Russo*.

I could see a lot more value in emblazoning my name over that building and my business than by being modest about using it.

There is a saying *fortune favours the brave*. And I have to say it smiled on me, but only after testing me out with a few frowns first.

Once in the building, we had enough courses to fill only three of the 12 floors.

But things were happening. We were winning Government tenders to run training courses for the unemployed.

Our training was good and high percentages of graduates from our courses succeeded in getting jobs, taking them off unemployment benefits.

The Government employment agency was impressed with this and continued to sign us up for a steady flow of contracts. As a result of this business growth and the further diversification and updating of the courses we were offering, we were able to expand our use of the building to six floors.

But six were still unoccupied.

To generate even more business, I decided to re-open an English course for international students.

I was apprehensive about doing this for a special reason associated with the June 1989 Tiananmen Square incident in Beijing, China.

Before that event, there had been a high level of interest among young people in China in enrolling for English and business training courses in Australia. My academy, and many other business colleges around Australia, had been accepting applications from thousands of students in China wishing to enrol in our courses.

The Chinese students were paying their fees in advance. Millions of dollars were flowing out of China into the bank accounts of the Australian educational institutions, including ours.

Some of those institutions were using this golden river of cash to buy buildings, and improve their facilities. Some were spending it in other ways.

We put the money we were receiving in a trust account – and thank God we did, because after Tiananmen Square it all had to be sent back, plus interest.

I could not take the credit for the foresight in putting the money we received into a trust account. It was Gerardo's idea. Ever the ethical lawyer, he insisted upon it.

Tiananmen Square put an end to the plans of all those Chinese students to come to Australia to study in our courses. Our government sent out an edict to all educational institutions that had been accepting enrolments. All fees that had been received had to be sent back to the students in China who had paid them – plus interest.

When I got this news I picked up the phone and dialled Gerardo's number and said to him: 'How come all your predictions happen to be right? The Government have just told us we have to send back the money. Thanks to you we can do it'.

So we sent all the fees we had received back to China – plus interest, a seven-figure amount. But many other institutions could not and got into terrible strife. Some English colleges were forced to close.

I sometimes wonder how I come to escape situations like that. If it had not been for Gerardo, I could have fallen into the same plight and lost my business. I said this to Gerardo, and he replied: 'Sarina, there is a natural law that seems to take care of those with good intentions. Think of all the people you have helped through your business. You have built up a lot of credits. This is your payback'.

After that event I lost my confidence in the international market, but having six empty floors, re-opening the English school was the best option for solving that problem.

Making that decision was one thing. Making it happen was another. To do so it was necessary to recruit multi-lingual people with academic as well as marketing skills. We chose well and before long we were enrolling students from Latin America, the Soviet Union, Europe, Scandinavia, Asia and South East Asia and the Pacific Islands.

The English classes occupied the top six floors. The building was now full. We were a happening organisation, and I had many good people on my staff to thank for it because you don't grow a business like ours without the commitment and dedication of talented people who share your vision.

A wonderful new opportunity opened up for the Russo organisation when the Government decided to privatise some of the activities of the

Commonwealth Employment Service (the CES) which was the government agency at which all unemployed people had to register to receive welfare payments. It was also the agency where businesses posted job vacancies for which unemployed people on the CES register could apply. Its mission was to reduce the unemployment rate by getting people into jobs, thereby saving the taxpayer dollars the government was paying out in welfare, but it wasn't doing all that well.

At the time of that privatisation decision, I was serving in an advisory capacity on a development committee set up by the Federal Department of Employment to work on issues relating to training for the unemployed.

I sensed there could be opportunities for my business in this new wave. I needed new people, so I went recruiting in the expectation that those opportunities would soon open up.

I was right. The Government called tenders for the outsourcing of the job matching, intensive assistance for long-term unemployed and job search training activities of the former CES. They called it Job Network. Fundamentally, it was a scheme to set up a network of privately-owned and operated employment agencies to help registered unemployed people find jobs. The government would pay these private agencies to process, train and gain employment for people on the unemployment register.

With our background in job skills training and job finding we were beautifully positioned to stake a claim for an agency contract. We had the connections, we had the infrastructure and we had the know-how.

We wrote a tender nominating eight suburbs of Brisbane and rural areas where we would establish offices. We won a contract to open up Job Network offices in each of those eight areas. The contracts were for 19 months, at the end of which it would be necessary to submit fresh tenders to retain the contract.

My business was now heading in a new direction. Perhaps this was what I had been working toward all along. From day one when I set up my typing school 19 years earlier I had made it my crusade to get my students into jobs that could give new meaning to their lives. That had been my drive, my passion. That passion had taken me on a long and fruitful journey. Incredibly, my school had blossomed into a large campus, the Russo Institute of Technology, teaching students from around Australia and around the world.

Now I was launching into a second major business – a fully-fledged recruitment and job-placement network. Was it destiny at work?

It was going to cost us a great deal of money to lease and fit out suitable offices in the eight locations we had won.

I threw myself into this project. I decided if I was to put so much money at risk in this new venture, I was going to drive it. I involved myself in the selection of the office sites and the design of their décor.

I wanted them to look smart, efficient and welcoming. I called our network of eight offices 'Sarina Russo Job Access Australia Pty Ltd' under the rationale 'think training, think how to get that job, *think Sarina Russo*'.

We hired 70 people to staff them and I vetted every individual. I wanted bright positive people with the will to succeed and I got them.

As the contracts approached their expiry dates, which were extended by two months, we geared up for a fresh round of tender submissions. Our success with the eight offices in the first wave of contracts encouraged us to believe we could go further afield into the states of NSW and Victoria.

To win additional sites outside the State of Queensland, to persuade the powers that be that our organisation was capable of delivering the results the Government wanted across such a large area of Australia, called for a huge effort in strategic thinking and detailed planning. We were pitching for what amounted to a seriously large contract.

Our tender covered every detail, anticipated every concern that might arise within the bureaucracy to which we were submitting. It was a huge document, an impressive tome that had absorbed hundreds of hours of work. We won 30 locations.

Having won the contract for 30 sites, we had to find office buildings, lease them, fit them out and recruit up to 200 new staff. We had only six weeks to do it, covering thousands of kilometres across three States of Australia.

The whole management team pitched in. It was an exhausting period for the Sarina Russo Group of companies.

I didn't want just any kind of office for my agencies. I wanted offices in prime parts of the cities and towns we were opening up in and I wanted those offices to be bright and welcoming with excellent facilities and strong branding on street level.

I wanted to offer the people who would be our clients excellent customer service. The environment I wanted them to come to had to be upbeat and stimulating.

We all worked at finding the right localities and Gerardo did the negotiating of the rental leases. Many of the candidates for the positions we were offering were former staff of the CES.

I knew the kind of people I wanted. They had to be able to share my vision, they had to demonstrate that they were not just average in the way they smiled, or shook hands, or answered the telephone. They had to have that passion and caring that lifted them up from average to excellent. I wanted teams of stars and I believe I have them.

Today, many of the agencies in our network are among the best perform-ing in the country. I find myself being invited to seminars and gatherings of other network providers to explain why we have been so successful. I am happy to share my 'secrets' because I want the privatised job network scheme to succeed.

I put our success down to hiring good people. I can't believe how lucky I am to have recruited such talented managers who have helped take us to the top in our field.

When I give thanks for my luck in my recruiting choices I always include Janet Vallino, who got me a job as a night school typing teacher in the first place. It was she who gave me the confidence to believe I could do it. Janet today works in the Sarina Russo Group of companies, specialising in training and education in recruitment methodologies and managerial techniques and practices.

My bank manager, Paul Anderson, once congratulated me on my recruiting successes.

He said, 'you know Sarina, you have amazing networking skills'. And referring to my key managers he said, 'you have this knack of knowing these people before you need them – and then they're there'.

In August 2001 when I was preparing for an overseas trip, little did I know how much I would need the commitment and support of those managers and everyone else in my organisation in the months ahead.

As I made my departure, it seemed that all the clouds in my world had silver linings. Business was great, I was bursting with energy – thanks to my fitness training – and I was looking forward to a fantastic time when I reached my destination.

I would never have caught that plane if I had known what awaited me at the end of my journey.

The Lessons

These are the key lessons I would like you to take from what I have written in Chapter Five:

1. Fear and failure are close together. Don't let fear cloud your judgement.

2. Accept the risk if you understand and accept the consequences of the worst-case scenario.

3. The pain of discipline weighs ounces. The pain of regret weighs tons.

4. When you are entrusted with other people's money, keep it safe and secure.

5. Have the final say in the recruitment of people for your business.

6. Ensure that the environment you have created for your clients is upbeat and stimulating.

7. Be available to give advice to others in your industry, to ensure its success as a whole.

CHAPTER SIX

What September 11, 2001 did to the world – and to me

The reason for my trip overseas in early September 2001 was to attend the Emmy Awards for outstanding achievement in television in the US. They were to be presented at a lavish ceremony in Hollywood on September 15. I had tickets through my membership of the Young Presidents' Association. All of my American YPO friends had been telling me what a wonderful occasion it was and I was really excited at the prospect of walking that famous red carpet for a night out with the stars. Representatives of the fashion and jewellery house Bulgari had invited me to wear jewellery from their fantastic range for this grand occasion and this made me feel really special

As I met YPO colleagues at a lovely Beverley Hills Hotel a few days before the awards, I couldn't help feeling how lucky I was. I would have so much to tell my friends and family – and my staff, with whom I always share the stories of my activities.

The buzz, the anticipation, the underlying excitement was so infectious I thought it would be hard to come down off the high I was feeling and get a good night's sleep.

I didn't know how true that was going to turn out to be.

I was out shopping on Rodeo Drive on September 10. At 2.00 p.m. – I'll never forget the time – I heard a rumbling sound and the ground beneath my feet was sending up frightening vibrations. Everyone around me froze.

My first thought was that there was a robbery in one of the stores. I saw objects in shop windows moving on the shelves. Some toppled over. The buildings were swaying! I knew what was causing it, but my mind would not accept it.

I was terrified. I turned and ran back to my hotel, where my worst fears were confirmed. There had been an earthquake. Was it the first of more to come? Wasn't there always an after-shock?

Being a regular visitor to the US, I closely follow their TV news programs. My mind flew back to reports I had seen of an earthquake in LA in 1994. Freeways and office buildings collapsed and houses were flattened and there were many casualties.

Oh my God, I thought, it's going to happen again and I'm right in the middle of it. I had a premonition of chaos and disaster. I had to get out of there. I emailed my office in Australia to tell them I was leaving LA to go to New York where I had many friends.

But I couldn't get a flight that day. I would have to wait overnight until the next day –September 11.

I went to bed in my hotel that night in my clothes. My bag was packed and my shoes were at the door. I slept in fits and starts. I was in an early morning doze when the phone rang.

When I became conscious of the ringing sound, I felt a stab of alarm. Was it happening? Was it an evacuation call?

I picked up the receiver and said in a shaky voice, 'hello'.

A voice I knew so well said, 'Hi … are you awake? … do you know what has happened? … turn on your TV.'

It was Marcello calling from Australia. I turned on my TV to see a vision of airliners crashing into the World Trade Center and the catastrophe that followed.

New York was under attack! Not only New York. The terrorists had also crashed an airliner into the Pentagon, the headquarters of the US Department of Defence, in Arlington, Virginia. They'd hijacked a fourth airliner for an attack on the White House, but brave passengers had fought the hijackers and all on board lost their lives when the plane crashed in Pennsylvania, thankfully short of its target.

My premonition of chaos and disaster had been right, but it wasn't caused by an earthquake. Terrorists were trying to destroy America.

I was almost hysterical. I snatched up the phone. 'Marcello, I'm coming home on the next flight,' I said.

'Sarina, that might be a problem. I'll do what I can from this end, but you might have to wait. Just try to stay calm and don't move from your hotel.'

Marcello was right. All flights in and out of America and across the country had been cancelled – and so were the Emmy Awards.

It was five days before I was able to get a flight back to Australia. I felt trapped and helpless. I was powerless and it felt awful. Money could not get me out of there – nor could influence or highly placed connections. I was just another individual on a long list.

I realised that in one terrible day I had lost the one thing I cherished most of all in life – my independence. I was still the same person I had been on September 10, my bank balance was the same, but I was now a prisoner of circumstances beyond my control. I was not accustomed to feeling helpless. My desire for independence had been the driving force of all my efforts to build a business. Now it was gone and that feeling of loss made me value it even more. I resolved that when I got out of there, when I got home, I was going to celebrate the independence that would then be returned to me.

I was cheered and touched by email messages of comfort and encouragement that I was receiving from my managers, staff and friends who knew I was in LA, including one message that said, 'don't worry Sarina. You will be ok. It's not your time to die. You have much more to achieve'.

I was not convinced – and nor would I be until my feet were firmly back on Australian soil.

I was able to phone my friends in New York and to my great relief they were all ok.

When flights to Australia resumed after the five-day grounding of all commercial air traffic, three flights were scheduled to Australia: one to Melbourne, one to Sydney and one to Brisbane. I normally fly business class or first class.

I was able to get a seat on the last flight of the first day of resumed services. But not business or first class – and not to my home city of Brisbane. All that was on offer was an economy class seat to Sydney. I didn't care. I took it.

There were huge queues at the airport, and an air of desperation. Everyone, including me, just wanted to get out of there ahead of the next catastrophe we all feared might happen.

I think every single person had the same desire and that was to see once more the face or faces of family and loved ones they had left behind and embrace them. When the plane was safely in the air there was a feeling of relief along with an edge of fear about potential hijackers.

I expected to be really emotional when I was back on Australian soil and reunited with my family in Brisbane but mostly I just felt numb. The first day back I had a lot of stories to tell and a lot of questions to ask about happenings during my absence – and then I went to bed and fell into a deep sleep.

On the second day of my return I went for a walk along the Brisbane river broadwalk, seeing all the familiar sights and smelling all the familiar, subtle smells the wind wafts off the river and its boat traffic. Walking along I suddenly burst into tears and could not stop. My emotions were mixed. It was such a wonderful relief to be home again in my beautiful city and it was also so awfully sad that the world had changed so terribly. I was sure it would never be the same again.

Those tears kept flowing all that day. I just could not stop for more than a few minutes at a time.

I felt I had to re-evaluate my life. I had to work out how this monstrous event would affect my business. It was not the time to make any major decisions. I postponed work on this book, which was then well advanced.

As President George Bush geared up his plans to go to war with the terrorists, I put overseas travel off the agenda. I made my marketing teams cancel excursions they had planned because I felt there was too much danger and I didn't want them to risk their lives. We go into the Middle East, Asia and many parts of Europe which were considered risk areas.

We lost business as a result, but I didn't care. The safety of my staff was my major concern.

It took several weeks for me to regain my confidence. My managers were extremely supportive. They understood how badly I had been shocked, but gently urged me to allow them to resume their overseas marketing expeditions. Among them was my nephew Andrew Pennisi, who is the International Marketing Manager of the Russo Institute of Technology. Andrew travels into the Middle East on student recruiting drives.

The Middle East is a difficult market for reasons of culture and language, but Andrew has built an affinity with a network of key people in the region, with the result that we have established an important source of business.

The anthrax mail scare, which extended into Australia, didn't make it any easier to let them go. What was the world coming to?

Everyone was affected by the terrorism of September 11 and the events that followed. Even if you were not personally involved in some way, you were still touched by them if you went to an airport and experienced the heightened security, hesitated opening your mail or found yourself looking over your shoulder a little bit more.

The world was on edge. We had all been reminded that no longer was there a really safe haven anywhere. And this changed people's thinking about their values. People were now placing more importance on being close to their families, on finding more meaning in their work, on enjoying small rituals like regular dinners with close friends, on finding pleasure in simple things. Life seemed more precious to all of us.

As I realised these things I decided that my role as a leader was to respond by creating a stable environment for my staff and a real sense of purpose, because purpose had been threatened by the events of September 11. In the weeks that followed September 11, business confidence in Australia recorded the largest drop in the history of surveys conducted by the National Australia Bank. All business sectors reported a large deterioration in the near term outlook.

The US economy was hit hard. Retail sales, consumer confidence and the production side of the economy were sent into a tailspin. Tourism was affected worst of all. Americans just stopped flying to overseas destinations and this had an enormous ripple effect on the international hospitality industry and downstream service providers like tour operators. One business that did boom, however, was flag-making. Americans everywhere sought to buy the Stars and Stripes to demonstrate their patriotism and their unity.

Australia's economy proved more resilient, despite the dive in confidence and events like the Ansett collapse, but it was still important to read the messages that were coming out of people's attitudes after September 11.

Customer service became more important than ever before. In those doubtful times people wanted certainty and reliability. They didn't want complications or stressful dealings. With the spectre of Osama Bin Laden and his al-Qaeda terrorist group stoking their fears, they were looking to have as much control as they possibly could over every aspect of their lives. They needed to know they were making correct choices.

As the weeks and the months went by and the next catastrophic terrorism event did not happen, and as Bin Laden and his al-Qaeda army were defeated in Afghanistan, people began to relax.

We entered a period of cautious normality but I don't think we can ever forget the message that September 11 has given us, that no longer is there a safe haven anywhere on earth. I sensed a new attitude in the people around me. There was a feeling that you should make the most of today, don't waste opportunities and don't hesitate to express your feelings to your friends and loved ones. I guess that was one good thing that came out of it.

I look back on the Year 2001 as the most harrowing of my life, but it was also a year in which I grew. I felt as if I had faced the worst and had survived. In fact our business results were excellent because our staff refused to be intimidated by the climate of fear.

It's strange how things work out. You strike the tough times and they can test you to your limits, but if you hang in there, if you hold your self-belief, it's amazing how things can turn around.

The year 2001 had certainly been a terrible trial. What would 2002 bring? I was due to attend a Harvard business course in January 2002, which meant a trip to New York. The prospect of flying overseas again was frightening, particularly to New York. I didn't think I would be able to go.

But somehow I conquered my fears and took that flight.

I am so thankful I did. That trip to New York marked the beginning of the most magical year of my life.

The Lessons

These are the key lessons I would like you to take from what I have written in Chapter Six:

1. Take action today rather than tomorrow

2. Make the most of today. Don't waste opportunities and don't hold back from expressing your feelings to friends and family.

3. Hang in there through the tough times. Hold your self-belief and things will turn around.

CHAPTER SEVEN

The most magical year of my life

It wasn't easy flying into New York. As we approached touchdown, my anxiety grew into a panic attack, but somehow I held myself together. In some strange way I felt like a pioneer travelling into unknown territory.

One of the first things I did after checking into my hotel was to visit the site of the terrorist attack – Ground Zero. I wept as I surveyed the flattened mess of the World Trade Center. I wept for the senseless loss of life and the madness that made it happen. So many wonderful, talented people had died in those twin towers. They were the movers and shakers of commerce in what I call the "engine of the world". That's what they all were, stock brokers, bankers, financiers, all the most brilliant brains, making it happen.

In 1998 I had ridden the express lift to the top of the North Tower with my nephew Marcello Pennisi. We wanted to experience the view up there from the restaurant known as the Windows on the World, occupying the 106th and 107th floors.

On the morning of September 11, 2001 that restaurant was the venue for a business seminar. All 79 staff and all of the guests died in the terror attack. My body started to shake as I thought about that – and of the day Marcello and I had dined there.

Marcello, who had graduated from university with a double degree – commerce and honours in law – was working with Ernst and Young in London in their Expatriate Private Client Services Department, and had flown in to New York to see me. He seemed to be set on a brilliant career. As we marvelled at the fantastic view of New York spread out below us, I said to him: 'Marcello, this is where you should aspire to be, in the engine of the world, with all the other great young minds that work here'.

Those words came back to me as I stood looking at the ruins in 2002. What if he had followed my advice? Would he have died here? The thought brought a fresh flood of tears to my eyes. Then I felt an overwhelming surge of gratitude for the hand of fate that had directed his path elsewhere. In fact, the growth of our business in 1999-2000 had been so great that we needed Marcello with us back in Australia. Since then he has proved his worth many times over as a senior executive in the Russo organisation and now serves as our legal counsel and Chief of Staff.

During that New York visit we had taken the ferry out to Ellis Island, the entry point to America for the 20 million migrants from Europe who were fleeing poverty, religious persecution or political unrest in their homelands in the early 1900s. The migrant reception building has now been converted to a museum containing records of all the migrants who were processed there.

They came to America on steamships. First class passengers were courteously inspected on ship before being transferred to New York. Only the steerage passengers were processed on Ellis Island. They had to answer 29 questions, giving their name, age, sex, marital status, occupation and race and nationality. They were asked about their ability to read or write, their physical and mental health, the money in their possession, prison record, if any, and whether they were polygamists or anarchists.

On one plaque inscribed with the names of Italian migrants who were processed there between 1910 and 1915 we counted the names of more than 300 Russos. We took photos of the migrant inscriptions and in the background of our photos, as we look at them today, are the Twin Towers.

In January 2002 it was difficult to turn my mind from the horror of the devastation at Ground Zero to the purpose of my visit to the US. Our studies at the Harvard Business School were clouded with the grief that still hung over New York only four months after the terrorist attack.

But there was also a mood of defiance among New Yorkers, a determination to carry on with life as it was before. Continuing to do all the normal things they did before September 11 was their way of fighting back. I was full of admiration for these brave, resilient New Yorkers.

In times of crisis it is wonderful how someone always seems to step forward to save the day. In New York, after September 11, that individual was Mayor Rudi Giuliani who was a pillar of strength in this shattered city.

It was he who urged them to carry on as normal and led by example, working tirelessly to get the city's utilities back into operation, taking every opportunity to boost people's spirits. He was so effective and inspiring in his leadership that America's most respected television star, Oprah Winfrey, invited him onto her show so that she could acknowledge him for what he had achieved.

Oprah paid this tribute to him: 'In the days and weeks following the attack, his composure, his grace under pressure and his efforts to offer hope and help to thousands in mourning earned him the name America's Mayor'.

In the defiant New York environment he had helped create, I was inspired to make the most of my study time this year.

The business lesson that came through to me was that for established businesses, this was a time to send out the message about your brand. The message should stress that you have been around a long time and that your brand represents reliable, high quality goods or services that customers can count on.

In this environment of uncertainty, the things that were most important to consumers were stability and continuance. Brands that stayed the same, and did not react wildly, would be the most attractive.

I think that this is a most important lesson. In times of uncertainty, give certainty to your customers. I would add one thing – there must also be certainty within the business and that must come from the attitude of its leader.

To me, New York is the most fascinating city in the world, full of amazing people doing amazing things and I snatched some time from my studies at Harvard to soak up its exciting atmosphere. In New York you never know who, or what, you will meet around the next corner.

One afternoon I entered a coffee shop on Madison Avenue with a friend. As we took our seats, our attention was drawn to a woman sitting alone. She was sobbing, almost hysterically.

'Are you ok?' I asked.

'I've had a terrible day,' she replied. 'My boyfriend has dumped me for another woman'.

I said, 'don't let that upset you. It happens to all of us. Besides, in New York there are thousands of eligible men'.

We calmed her down and invited her to join us. After she had got the story of her ex-boyfriend off her chest, we got to talking about Australia. It turned out that she knew people in Sydney who were also acquaintances of mine.

Before we parted I invited her to call me if she felt she needed someone to talk to because it was obvious she had been deeply hurt. She called me the very next day and said that because we had helped get her through her terrible day she would like me to meet a friend who had entrée to important New York social events.

The friend turned out to be Kathy Sloane, a highly-connected real estate professional who had struck up a friendship with Bill and Hillary Clinton while helping them to find a home to buy in New York after his Presidency ended and Hillary entered the race to win a seat in the US Senate representing the state of New York.

Kathy had many fascinating stories about New York and its movers and shakers. She invited me to attend a function at which Hillary Clinton was to pay tribute to two theatre people who had produced the musical *Chicago*.

I was delighted to accept this invitation. I have long been an admirer of Hillary Clinton, not only for the way she distinguished herself as First Lady during her husband's Presidency, but for her work for children's education throughout her career. And I loved the story Bill Clinton has related in a number of interviews of how they met. She walked up to him in the Library at the Yale Law School, where they were both students and said: 'If you're going to keep staring at me, I might as well introduce myself'.

I had run into Bill Clinton at the Wimbledon tennis finals in 2001. We were a few rows apart and as an admirer of his achievements in his term as President I couldn't resist calling out, *Australia loves you, Mr President.* He had come over to shake my hand and thank me for the remark. His words to me were: *'It was an honour to serve.'*

The coincidence was that at the time I heard Hillary speak – and I enjoyed her speech immensely – he was due to visit Brisbane in a couple of months to give one of his peace speeches. My business was buying corporate tickets for the dinner at which he was to give the speech.

In fact the coincidence got even greater. Not long after I attended that function with Hillary, the Sarina Russo Group was invited to bid for the naming rights of the Clinton dinner in Brisbane. The company that submitted the closest bid to the $110,000 asking price would win the rights.

We decided to go for it. Aside from the opportunity to win publicity for the Russo organisation and its businesses, I had a special reason for wanting to meet and talk with the 42nd President of the United States – and the naming rights would give me that opportunity because I would be at his side at the dinner table.

Through my annual visits to the Harvard Business School during his Presidency I had come to admire him for his wonderful intellect, his humanitarianism, for his focus on education and employment opportunities for people at all levels of society. They were my interests too.

But there was another reason. I had read about the peace speech he was giving to audiences around the world, that delivered hope in overcoming terrorism and presented a vision of fostering the interdependence of nations to bridge the gap between the warring factions of the planet. Because of my experience in the US in September 2001 I responded to that message with passion.

If I could do something to endorse and help spread that message I wanted to do so. We put in a bid and won the naming rights. I was delighted – and excited that the people of Brisbane would be able to hear this former world leader present his vision of a better world. Moreover, the dinner was to help raise funds for the Royal Children's Hospital, a cause dear to my heart.

I invited Kathy Sloane to fly out from New York to be my guest at the dinner and she accepted.

When Bill Clinton came to Brisbane to give his speech, his third in Australia after speeches in Perth and Melbourne, there was a fierce demand for tickets. It was a gala night at the Sheraton Hotel as 750 people gathered in their finery in the grand ballroom to await his arrival.

I waited outside the ballroom, with Queensland Premier Peter Beattie, to meet the President on his arrival. Before he made his entrance to the ballroom we accompanied him on a tour of a display of memorabilia which was to be auctioned for charity at the end of the evening.

He fell in love with a still shot from the movie Casablanca starring Humphrey Bogart and Ingrid Bergman. The photograph was signed by both stars. He told me that he and his wife Hillary had seen the movie when they were dating as university students and that the photo brought back wonderful memories of their romance. I decided to buy it for him in the silent auction and later, when I presented it to him, he said he would give it to Hillary as a gift from Australia.

Outside the ballroom he accidentally stepped on the train of my dress and said, "Sarina, walk beside me". I was overwhelmed.

So when he made his grand entrance, I was at his side in the glittering silver lamé evening gown that had been designed for me by Brisbane couturier Richard De Chazel. The 750 guests were on their feet, clapping and cheering as we marched to the main table.

As we stepped through the doorway I heard the introduction, *"President Bill Clinton with Sarina Russo"*. It felt as if I was a star in a movie ... all of that thunderous applause and me sharing the spotlight with the President. I thought *My God ... is this really happening to me, or am I dreaming?'*.

Other guests at the main table included Peter Beattie and his wife Heather and the Lord Mayor of Brisbane, Jim Soorley and his partner Mary Philip, along with senior executives of the Sarina Russo Group, business leaders and friends.

The President made us feel so relaxed. At one stage Heather Beattie was speaking to her son Matthew over her mobile phone. The President took the phone from her and said to the 13-year-old at the other end, "Hi. I am President Bill Clinton" and then proceeded to chat with him. Imagine how that boy felt when he heard those words.

In a briefing before the dinner my nephew, Marcello Pennisi had said to me: "Remember Sarina, this is an evening with Bill Clinton, not a dinner with Bill Clinton".

I said, "You mean he does not eat?" He said, "No, he does not eat."

But when the entrée arrived, the President said to the waitress, "That looks nice. I will have one".

I said, "Mr President, I understood you don't have dinner at these functions. He said, "That's correct, but I will join you tonight."

The entrée was all he ate – and all I ate.

It was my scheduled duty to introduce the President before his speech, but Sydney radio celebrity Alan Jones, who was MC for the evening, beat me to it with a 15-minute oration about the President's career.

In the expectation that he would simply introduce me to the guests to make my scheduled three-minute introduction, I was standing at the foot of the steps leading up to the podium as Jones worked through his 13-page speech.

It felt like hours. I said to myself, "My God, what is left for me to say?". But I was determined. I had been waiting and preparing for this moment and I was not going to let this put me off.

Finally I got possession of the podium and made my short speech. At the end of it I presented the President with a didgeridoo from northern Queensland. He pulled it out of its cover and disappointed the guests when he did not blow into it.

As a member of the host committee I was invited, along with Clinton family friend Kathy Sloane, to attend the Clinton dinner in Sydney the following night. I had been so overwhelmed by his speech in Brisbane that I felt I could not miss the opportunity to hear it again. It was a truly inspirational oration and I believe so deeply in its message about building world peace through creating an interdependence of nations that I have included extracts from it in the next chapter.

The Sydney visit turned out to be a continuous round of functions with the President, not only the Saturday night dinner attended by 2200 people, but also a Sydney Harbour cruise with the President and a restricted guest list of 30, and then a private party for those associated with the organisation of the Clinton dinners in Australia.

We were to have lunch with the President and his entourage at the Australian Club on Sunday but it was cancelled because of time constraints. Kathy and I were invited to join the group following the President on his round of golf at the Club and we enjoyed our electric buggy ride around the course as spectators of the President and his playing partners.

We were also among the privileged few who farewelled him from Sydney and received his thanks for our support and hospitality. His advisor carried the didgeridoo and the Casablanca photograph onto the plane on behalf of the President.

I had two more encounters with the President in 2002 – in New York, where he was given a peace award in April and in New Zealand in May where he had a round table discussion in a closed session with 20 Australian and New Zealand business leaders.

I was Kathy Sloane's guest in New York. When he spotted me among the arrivals at the peace function attended by 800 New Yorkers, he looked surprised and said, *'Sarina – what are you doing here?'*.

I replied: 'I'm here to support you, Mr President'.

He leaned forward to kiss me on the cheek, and as he did so he brushed a pearl earring I was wearing and it fell to the floor. As it fell, he moved on without noticing what had happened.

I didn't care that I was in the midst of the cream of New York society. I was not going to lose that pearl – or have it crushed under someone's heel. I dropped to my hands and knees and found it. You can imagine the looks on the faces of the other guests in the vicinity when this woman who had been greeted so warmly by the President was suddenly scrabbling around on the floor. Their faces cleared when I stood up and re-attached my earring.

The President told us, at the New Zealand round table meeting, that 30 per cent of his time was taken up in personal activities, 20 per cent working for charity and 50 per cent working in public service. His public service activities include helping people in places like India and Africa and developing trusts to help fight various diseases. His goal for 2004-05 was to divide his time so that he spent 30 per cent on personal activities and 70 per cent in public service.

I was delighted when I was invited to attend this closed discussion with him in Wellington, New Zealand, in May as one of 20 Australian and New Zealand business leaders. I just wanted to hear more about his vision of world interdependence which was of special interest to me for two reasons: one was that our business reaches into many parts of the world, including third world countries and the other was the terror I had experienced in the US around September 11, 2001.

The President expanded on his beliefs of interdependence. It's a long word, so what does it mean?

Through our round-table discussions with him – and our less formal chats with him as he relaxed in a cigar bar after our round-table session – I came to an understanding of what he means by it.

Interdependence is about making allies. It's about nations having a dependence on each another for certain things so that there is a mutual benefit. It's about forming partnerships, forming connections between nations and creating a flow of assistance from prosperous nations to poorer nations. He believes the path to interdependence is to be able to see things clearly, to understand the problems of other nations, to respect their culture and beliefs and to see both sides of a situation in a spirit of determination to achieve sympathetic understanding.

In his speech he paints two contrasting pictures of the world. He cleverly does this by describing what people from the prosperous countries of the world might nominate as the most important issue of the 21st century and then describing what the people of the poorest countries would nominate as their most important issue of the century.

The differences in the answers are devastating, as you will read in the extracts from his speech in the next chapter. They give you a totally new perspective of the world we live in and where it is headed.

His analysis of the world as it had been before September 11, his comments on the reality of the world as it is today and his assessment of its future as a global village were presented with such insight and wisdom that I was convinced that as an educator I must do all that I can to ensure that as many of our Australian teachers and professors as possible have the opportunity to hear him first hand. I understand he will be returning to Australia within the next year and I am planning to work with all those involved as hosts and organisers to incorporate an educational component in his visit.

There is probably no single voice that is more eloquent, inspirational and convincing on the obligations that go with world interdependence than Bill Clinton's. To have met him, to have spoken to him one-on-one and to have listened, in different forums, to the brilliance of his analysis of the world's problems was a memorable – no, magical – experience.

He radiates optimism, confidence and a kind of shining wisdom. Spending some time with him leaves you charged with positive energy. I have no doubt that he is one of the great political minds of American history.

Meeting him has made me think how amazing life can be. Which one of my teachers would have predicted that the little migrant Sicilian girl, who was one of their problem students in their English classes, would one day be hosting an American president at a grand dinner, and getting to know him on a first name basis?

Somewhere in Australia right now I am sure there is another child (or children) struggling to fit in, as I struggled, and who one day will amaze all the people who doubted them by achieving great success through an awakening power of self belief.

One of the things that Bill Clinton shared with us in New Zealand was that he felt his career had been like a bungy jump, but through all the ups and downs he has always remained positive.

As he put it, anyone can want something, but it is those who believe in their goals that achieve.

Somebody once said to me that the best form of revenge is massive success. That is not to say that revenge is worth seeking, but the discovery of the power of self-belief and the application of it to pursue goals certainly is worth seeking.

I am proud of my success, but in Paris a few weeks after hosting the Clinton dinner in Brisbane I felt humble as I took my place among other businesswomen from around the world to be acknowledged as one of the 40 leading women entrepreneurs of the world for 2002.

Usually I am surrounded by men who are super achievers. At Harvard Business School, for example, our classes are made up of 150 men and 12 women. Most of the organisations I do business with are led by men.

But, in Paris, I was just one of a host of women who were super-achievers in an amazing diversity of businesses, including agriculture, banking, bottling, communications, construction, cosmetics, engineering, fashion, finance, mining, health care, import/export trading, manufacturing, publishing, real estate, service industries, textiles, transport and travel.

As I mingled with these women and heard their success stories, my feelings were mixed. I was both humble to be there among them and I also felt proud to be a woman.

The Leading Women Entrepreneurs of the World concept was created by the Star Group, a US based global corporation that provides consulting services to corporations, associations and government entities around the world. An independent selection committee reviews and assesses nominations sent in from all around the world before choosing 40 women to be honoured as leading women entrepreneurs of the world for a particular year.

Hundreds of names are submitted by business leaders and women's organisations in 68 countries. Names are also drawn from the databases of universities, libraries and major consulates spanning 72 countries.

My nomination was sent in by another Queensland woman business achiever, Betty Bryne Henderson, who took over her husband's Ford dealership after his death, and built it into the largest in Queensland. She herself was nominated and chosen as a leading woman entrepreneur in a previous year.

Anita Alberts, President of the Star Group who sadly died of cancer a few months after the 2002 awards, explained that her company created the concept of an annual gala to celebrate the selection of leading women entrepreneurs of the world to highlight the accomplishments of women business owners worldwide, the effect they have on the global economy and especially to showcase them as role models of success for the next generation.

I was one of 10 women chosen to tell the stories of their successes (and failures) in television interviews that were to be screened on cable TV in America.

It was a fairytale experience to be there. We all felt like princesses as we were fêted at different gala functions in two different French castles, the

Chateau de Montvillargenne and Chateau de Chantilly. Dignitaries of France and of the United Nations Children's Fund, which is supported by the Leading Women Entrepreneurs of the World movement, were in attendance along with many of the 280 businesswomen who had been chosen as leading women entrepreneurs in previous years.

In recognition of our induction to the honour roll, each of us was presented with an exquisitely designed white gold gingko leaf pin displaying a beautiful Paspaley (Australia) South Sea Pearl.

There is a story behind the creation of this gift. In 2000, Paspaley Pearls of Australia committed to sponsorship of the Leading Women Entrepreneurs event held in Madrid in 2001.

Marilynne Paspaley, one of the principals of the family firm, told me she thought it would be exciting to invite Carrera y Carrera, a Spanish company considered to be one of the leading jewellers in the world, to work with Paspaley to create a pin that was a fitting symbol of achievement for the women being honoured.

In discussing what would be appropriate, the two firms agreed that the gingko tree and leaf seemed to symbolise characteristics required in building a successful business –longevity, strength, clarity of mind and passion.

The gingko leaf has been used for centuries in eastern medicine because of its properties which clear the brain, stimulate blood flow and strengthen the system.

In explaining why she felt the gingko leaf and a pearl pin would be a perfect award to give the women entrepreneurs, Marilynne told me: 'Due to its rarity, the pearl in all ancient cultures has been held in high esteem as a sign of power and status, as well as a statement of one's appreciation of aesthetics. Its natural beauty has made it the symbol of femininity and love.

'The two motifs combined, the gingko leaf and the South Sea pearl, epitomised for me the regard in which I hold these women. I wanted to create a pin that was worthy of their achievements. I believe I have done so.'

I agree. The pin is 18ct white gold and each pearl was hand-picked by Marilynne Paspaley. Each of the 40 pins presented in Paris had been moulded to the unique shape and size of each pearl, as every pearl was slightly different, and consequently every pin was slightly different.

Paspaley have had a business relationship with Carrera y Carrera for more than 15 years, and are the exclusive stockists of Carrera y Carrera in Australia. Over the years, the two firms have collaborated on designs by Carrera which have been exclusive to Paspaley.

As I listened to the speeches in Paris reflecting on the vision of Anita Roberts, the founder of the Leading Women Entrepreneurs movement, to create a sisterhood of the most powerful and influential women on earth to act as a force for good, my mind was drawn back to the words of Bill Clinton about achieving world peace through interdependence.

I felt as if fate had put me in a position where I was obliged to find a way to use my talents to support their causes, which are really one and the same thing.

Anita Roberts said to us at that Paris ceremony: 'In this world utterly trembling from terrorism now, I can ideally foresee all of you Leading Women Entrepreneurs of the World waging peace in each of your countries. There are now 280 of you in over 60 countries.

'Each of you must mobilise all the women and resources in your own country. We want peace in this world – and the leading women entrepreneurs of the world can be the peacemakers.'

To me there was a connection between that statement and the following statement Bill Clinton made in his peace speech – *It's important that we do more to build the pool of potential partners in the world and shrink the pool of potential terrorists'.*

Now, as a member of this sisterhood of leading women entrepreneurs I have been invited to participate in Harvard University's global program entitled *Women and Power: Leadership in a New World.* This movement incorporates the university's Women Waging Peace, Women World Leaders and Women's Leadership Board programs.

As I said in my introduction to this book, I feel good about having been inducted into that sisterhood and I am grateful for the opportunity to make some contribution towards achieving its objectives. There will be joy not only in making some advances but also in working with such wonderfully talented people who have been lifetime achievers.

The Lessons

These are the key lessons I would like you to take from what I have written in Chapter Seven:

1. In times of uncertainty your customers want stability and continuance.

2. Carrying on as normal is a morale-boosting way of fighting back against terrorism.

3. Be supportive to strangers in distress.

4. Be open to meeting new people and sharing new experiences.

5. No matter who you are, or how old you are you, too, may one day dine with a President.

CHAPTER EIGHT

The message of Bill Clinton

Bill Clinton may no longer hold the power of executive office, but this former President is a on a grand mission to create a more peaceful and understanding world by using the power he continues to hold – the peacemaker legacy he took from his term as 42nd President, his grasp of world affairs, his intellect and his stunning oratory skills. In 14 months, through 2001 and 2002, he made 200 speeches in more than 30 countries, all on the theme of reaching for peace through an interdependence of nations.

I have included in this book the following extracts from the peace speech he makes around the world in the hope that they will help spread the enlightenment he seeks to bring through his speaking.

On terrorism, he says:

'Terror, the killing of non combatants for economic, political or religious reasons has a very long history – as long as organised combat itself. And yet it has never succeeded as a military strategy standing on its own...'

He cites incidences of terror and atrocities back through the centuries, committed by nations of all races and political and religious beliefs and goes on to say:

'...It is troubling when 5000 people die, not in some faraway battlefield, but in downtown New York (and seen) on television. But you have to recognise that unless this is something different than has ever occurred in human history, we will figure out how to defend ourselves and civilisation will endure...

'...you cannot be paralysed by this. No terrorist strategy has ever prevailed. People who want to damage always win, in the beginning, but people always figure out defences. And the ultimate purpose of terrorism is not to win military victories anyway, but to terrorise, to make you afraid to get up in the morning, afraid of the future and afraid of each other...

'.... I met an Egyptian the first day I went down to see the people in the Crisis Centre after September 11. This big Egyptian fellow with tears in his eyes said, "I'm an Egyptian Muslim American, and I hate what happened probably worse than you do and I'm so afraid my fellow Americans will never trust me again"...

'...That's what they (the terrorists) want.'

On the state of the world, he tells his audience:

'It's not enough to win the fight we're in. It's important that we do more to build the pool of potential partners in the world and shrink the pool of potential terrorists. And that has nothing to do with the fight we're in. It has to do with what else we do, and that depends basically on how you analyse the world. I've been going all over the world and I've been going all over America going through this exercise so I'll take you through it.'

Then he asks his audience to try to remember how they viewed the world on September 10th before the terrorist attack.

'If I had asked you on that day, "what is the single most dominant element of the 21st century world what would your answer have been"?.'.

He suggests that people in prosperous western cultures might have answered, *'the global economy'*.

He explains: 'The globalisation of the economy is the most dominant element because it's made America 22 and a half million jobs and it's lifted more people out of poverty in the last 30 years than were ever lifted out in all human history'.

Alternatively, he suggests some people might have answered, *'the information technology revolution, because that's what has given us all the productivity that has driven the economic growth'*.

He elaborates: 'When I became President in January 1993, there were only 50 sites on the worldwide web. When I left office there were 350 million. In eight years. Today, before the anthrax scare, there were 30 times as many messages transmitted by email as the postal services every day in America'.

He suggests a third answer might have been: *'The most significant thing about the early 21st century will be the advances in biological science'*.

He tells his audience: 'It will rival the significance of the discovery of DNA. It will rival the significance of Newtonian physics. We sequenced the human genome; we're developing microscopic testing methods. Soon we'll be able to identify cancers when they're just a few cells in size. Soon we'll be able to give young mothers gene cards to take home with their newborn babies. In countries with good health systems, children will have life expectancies in excess of 90 years'.

Another answer that might have come out in a free, prosperous culture, he said, was: *'The most important thing about the modern world is the growth of democracy and diversity, because that is the environment within which all the economic growth, all the technological growth and all the scientific advances flourish best'*.

Again, he elaborates: 'I was honoured to be president at the first time in history when more than half the world's people lived under governments of their own choosing and when America, and other advanced countries, became far more diverse racially, ethnically and religiously than ever before and the societies were actually working, and working better – and, I might add, a lot more interesting because of our diversity'.

Then the President asks his audience to think about how the people in poor countries might have answered if they had been asked on September 10 what was the single most dominant element of the 21st century world.

He outlines four probable answers.

He says one might have been: *'Global poverty will dominate the early 21st century because half the world's people aren't in the global economy'.*

'A billion people live on less than a dollar a day,' he tells his audience. 'A billion and a half people never get a clean glass of water and one woman dies every minute in childbirth. And that's a recipe for explosion and that will dominate the world.'

He suggests a second answer might have been: *'The environment crisis will consume us. The shortage of water, the deterioration of the oceans from which we get our oxygen and, most all, global warming'.*

He explains: 'If the earth warms for the next 50 years at the rate of the last 10, we'll lose fifty feet of Manhattan Island and the Florida Everglades I worked so hard to save. Whole Pacific Island nations will be flooded and tens of million food refugees will be created, destabilising governments and causing violence'.

A third answer might have been: *'Before global warming gets us, the epidemics will'.*

He elaborates: 'All over the world, public health systems are crashing down and just to take AIDS as an example, there are now over 36 million cases and 22 million have already died. If we don't turn the trend around there will be 100 million AIDS cases in five years, making it the worst epidemic since the Plague swept Europe in the 14th century and killed one in four people. The fastest-growing rates are in the Soviet Union, on Europe's back door and the second fastest-growing rates are in the Caribbean on America's front door and the third fastest-growing rates are in India, the biggest democracy in the world. And the Chinese just admitted they had twice as many cases as they previously thought and only four per cent of the adults in our biggest nation know how AIDS is contracted and spread. So today, two thirds of the cases are in Africa. Tomorrow it's everybody's problem unless we turn it around'.

Then he gives one final alterative answer.

'You might have said, even on September 10th, "no, no, even before the health crises we will be consumed by terrorism, by the marriage of modern weapons of destruction to ancient racial, religious and tribal hatreds".'

And that brings him to his vision for peace.

He invites his audience to stack up the positive things he mentioned – the global economy, the explosion of information technology, the biological science advances and democracy and diversity – against the negative things – the global poverty, the environmental crisis, the health crises and the terror.

He asks: 'What do all eight of those things have in common? They all reflect the absolutely breathless increase in global interdependence, the extent of which the barriers of national borders don't count for much anymore, and to which we are all affected by things that happen a long way from home.

'Things that used to happen a long way from home can now happen next door.

'In other words. I honestly believe it's very important if you want to understand the world in which you live that you see September 11 as the dark side from all the benefits we've gotten from tearing down the walls, collapsing the distances and spreading the information that we have across the world.

'We have not changed human nature, we have not solved all the problems and there are a lot of people who see the world differently than we do.

'You cannot collapse walls, collapse differences and spread information without making yourself more vulnerable to forces of destruction.'

Speaking about solutions, he says: 'We have to look ahead and say, ok, we'll win this fight we're in (in Afghanistan) but we also have to create a world in which we have more partners and fewer potential terrorists.

'And how are we going to do that? We have to spread the benefits and shrink the burdens of the 21st century world, number one. Number two, we have to deal with the fact that most terrorists come from places that are not democracies. And number three is that we have to deal with the special challenges presented in the Muslim world, because Islam is our fastest-growing religion (in America) and we have to lift up the positive forces there and encourage those with enough courage to stand up for them ...

'...This is a struggle to define the soul of the 21st century. We have to win the fight we're in but we also have to create more partners and reduce the terrorist pool.

'So what do we have to do?

'First we have to reduce poverty and create more economic opportunity. In 2000 we relieved the debt of the poorest countries. We ought to do more of it because we only relieved the debt if they put money to education, health care, or economic development to make sure the money wouldn't be wasted. And the stories are stunning, what's being done with the money in those countries. We should do more of that.

'In 2000 we gave two million micro enterprise loans to poor people in Asia, Latin America and Africa. We ought to be giving twenty million a year or more. They average fifty or sixty dollars apiece. They put a lot of poor village people in business. We should do more. A lot cheaper than going to war.

'Second thing we ought to do is get the kids of the world in school. There are a hundred million children who never go to school. In a poor country, one year of school is worth ten per cent to twenty per cent increased income for life. In my last year as President we got 300 million dollars to feed six million children a good meal every day for a year, but only if they went to school. It was amazing. Kids were flooding into schools who didn't go before because they came from families that didn't have the ability to give them a good meal every day. This is a lot cheaper than going to war and it makes a big difference.

'Same argument applies to AIDS. UN Secretary General Kofi Annan asked for seven billion dollars a year for a global fund to fight infectious diseases. I've done a lot of work in this area. We can turn this epidemic around in three years. Brazil cut the death rate in half in three years with medicine and prevention. Uganda, with no medicine, cut the death rate in half in five years. We do not have to have 100 million AIDS cases in five years. Fledgling democracies will be destroyed by this. They will not be able to sustain an AIDS caseload of 100 million. And we don't have to have it happen. We ought to fund this problem. It's not very much money.'

On **global warming**, he says: 'We could actually make money out of that and so could the developing world. There's a trillion dollar untapped market for alternative energy and energy conservation technologies are available right now. All we have to do is help finance it... I think this is really important. If we do these things we will create a more positive interdependent world'.

On **democracy** he says: 'We must do more about democracy. Ten years ago I said it ought to matter to us how people govern themselves because democracies, by and large, do not go to war with each other, don't sponsor terrorist acts against each other and are more likely to be reliable partners, protect the environment and abide by the law. Democracy is a stabilising force. It provides non-violent means of resolving disputes.

I believe that. And it's no accident that most of these terrorists come from 'non-democratic countries'.

He says we have to recognise that special challenges are presented by the Muslim world in which people go into Mosques and demonise Americans, the West, Christianity and Jews.

'A lot of these folks have been our friends, America's friends and my friends. But we have created a discordant world in which it's hard to sort out who is where. And we've now reached a point with all these people lying dead and these terrorist threats, with the anthrax and everything, where people need to actually say what it is they believe.

'And we need to do a better job of getting the facts out. Most Muslims in the Middle East, I'll guarantee, don't know that the last time we used military power was to protect poor Muslims in Bosnia and Kosovo ... most people in the Middle East have forgotten, if they did know, that it was America that advocated the establishment of a Palestine state and reconciliation with Israel which would protect both sides' equities in Jerusalem. Now we're not for running Israel out of the Middle East. If that's what they want they ought to say that, but don't pretend that America has not been sensitive to the legitimate aspirations of Palestinians. It's not true.

'And I think in America we need to do more to give courage and give voice to our vibrant Muslim community of people that are anti-terror. In New York these young people came up to me and said they were proud to be Muslims and proud to be living in America. One was Egyptian, one was Pakistani and they just hated all this terrorism. They ought to be given courage and identified and given support to stand against this.'

He sums up by saying: 'This is not a perfect society, but it is one that is stumbling in the right direction. When you strip everything I have said down to one sentence, it basically comes down to this: ever since civilisations began, people have fought with their own inner demons over whether what we have in common is the most important thing about life, or whether our differences are the most important thing about life. That's what all this comes down to...

'... No terrorist campaign has ever succeeded and this one won't if you don't give it permission. You can have the most exciting time in our history, but we have to defeat people who think they can find redemption in our destruction. Then we have to be smart enough to get rid of our arrogant self-righteousness so that we don't claim for ourselves things we deny others.

'Then in the end we've got to be able to stand up and say we are not against Islam, but we want to have a clear understanding about what we think is the nature of truth, the value of life and the content of community. If we do that, you will still live in the best time the world has ever known.'

The above extracts represent the bare skeleton of his speech. As compelling as it is to read, it is even more compelling to hear because the President's delivery is spell-binding.

It is my belief that repetition is the mother of skill. If you keep hearing something over and over again you can only become a master yourself. I believe that if Bill Clinton continues to deliver his message to audiences around the world over and over again, the good things he advocates will one day be achieved.

The Lessons

These are the key lessons I would like you to take from Chapter Eight:

1. Be inspired by the message of Bill Clinton to open your mind to what's happening around the world.

2. Be inspired by the message of Bill Clinton to care more about the poor people of the world.

3. Be inspired by the message of Bill Clinton to try to understand the attitudes of people of different religious, racial and cultural backgrounds.

CHAPTER NINE

The lessons of my life

As I look back on 2002 I find it difficult to believe that so many powerful new influences entered my life in such a short space of time. I was profoundly influenced by the philosophy of Bill Clinton and in Paris, at the Leading Women Entrepreneur awards, I came into contact with kindred spirits who made me see myself in a new light.

I realised I was not an 'abnormal' woman with some kind of freakish quality that had made me a business success. I was not so different. There were many other women like me who thought much the same way, who were driven by similar ambitions and emotions and they came from all kinds of cultural backgrounds and industries.

It was so liberating. I got to know a few of the other leading entrepreneurs really well. Francine le Frek, who was chosen as a leading woman entrepreneur because of her success in the entertainment industry, became a good friend.

Francine has won Toni Awards and Emmy Awards as a TV producer. She lives in New York. I admired her enormously. Even though she came from a rich family, she went out on her own to do her own thing. And her family is not just rich, but super rich. Her father is a billionaire in the construction industry.

She continues to be a source of inspiration to me. We talk on the phone every second day.

Another new influence in my life was Martin Luther King III. He came to Brisbane in May to speak at the 2002 Dinner For Reconciliation, in the Plaza Terrace Ballroom at the Brisbane Convention and Exhibition Centre. The Sarina Russo Group were invited to purchase corporate tables for this dinner, part of the proceeds of which were to be presented to the reconciliation movement in Queensland.

I was glad to support their cause and we purchased two tables.

Martin Luther King III is another inspiring speaker, carrying on his father's *I Have A Dream* crusade to bring equality and justice for all people.

We were stirred by this man's recollection of his father's famous *I Have A Dream* oration.

> *I have a dream my four little children will one day live in a nation where they will not be judged by the colour of their skin, but by the content of their character. I have a dream today.*
>
> *I have a dream that one day little black boys and black girls will be able to join hands with little white boys and white girls as sisters and brothers. I have a dream today.*

In his pursuit of that dream, his father won the Nobel Peace Prize, but three years after receiving it he was gunned down by an assassin as he stood leaning over the balcony of the Lorraine Motel in Memphis, Tennessee.

Martin Luther King III is carrying on his father's crusade, but on a global scale. He was a key figure in creating the Africa Initiative, a program developed to end starvation in Africa. In the 1980s he campaigned for the freedom of Nelson Mandela and in the 1990s he campaigned to establish order in troubled third world nations like Haiti and Nigeria.

I was deeply moved by his speech. I consider it a privilege to have met him and spoken with him. I was also strengthened by the knowledge that there are people of such extraordinary talent like him, Bill Clinton and, until her death, Anita Roberts, dedicating themselves to righting the wrongs of the world and evening up the differences in such inspiring ways.

In 2001 I was absolutely shattered by my experiences in the US around September 11. My mother lived through World War II while my father was away with the Italian army. For a while after September 11, I thought that it was going to happen again – another world war.

But as I look back on the past two years, the dark clouds that I feared have melted away and I now see sunny skies. I have come to feel really comfortable with who I am. I have a sense of purpose, a sense of achievement, a sense of knowing who I am, and I draw strength from an inner confidence that my intuition, my emotional intelligence is a powerful tool for me.

I have completed my 10th annual study visit to Harvard Business School and I now feel that I should go to another University to experience a different type of educational experience.

I am still a go-go, high energy achiever, but I have become more reflective about life. The shock of the sudden death of a dear friend and a man of enormous talent, has really had an impact on me. His name was Bernie Green and he was only in his early 50s when he died from a massive heart attack a few days after I had lunch with him. We discussed his future at that lunch because he was facing the prospect of a career change.

Bernie's death crystallised for me the realisation that what life is all about is simply *living* and cherishing loved ones and friends. It's all about enjoying the journey that is called life. What really is important is that the people you love are still around you. Life is just so precious.

I loved an interview with Art Linkletter on the Larry King show on CNN, when Art turned 90. Larry asked: 'What in your life have you thought was incredible? Was it the space age, was it the computer age?'

Art replied: 'No, it's *my* age. The people who were born in my era are all dead and I've been given an extra 30 years of life that a lot of people haven't had. To me that has been the most precious thing in my life'.

And Art Linkletter, who is beloved in America for his wonderful sense of humour, has crammed so much into his 90 years. As a radio and television personality for more than 60 years he was nominated for the Emmy Awards several times and twice won an Emmy. He also won a Grammy award. He wrote 23 books, including one of the top 14 best sellers in American publishing history, entitled *Kids Say The Darndest Things*. His latest book, *Old Age Is Not for Sissies* was also an American best seller. He represented the US as Goodwill Ambassador at Australia's bi-centennial celebrations.

I'll never forget his answer to that question, because what it tells me is that when it comes down to it, it's not just about business, it is all about life.

Life is not just about living to the fullest each day, it is also about holding on to your life by looking after yourself .

I watch my diet, I restrict my alcohol intake and I get plenty of exercise, swimming and jogging. I jog 7 kilometres five days a week with a personal trainer. In June this year I ran once again in Brisbane's 12 kilometre Bridge to Brisbane event in which there were more than 5000 runners. My time this year was 78 minutes, an improvement of two minutes on my time in 2001.

I can't boast about it because my nephew Mark Berlese also ran and completed the course in 52 minutes, 26 minutes faster than me – and he had a bruised foot from a soccer clash! I have to say that Mark, who is the Operations Manager of the Russo Institute of Technology, is an absolute inspiration in terms of health and fitness. He ran in Sydney's City to Surf a week later and completed the 14 kilometres in 62 minutes, finishing in the first 2000 of the 63,000 runners.

Mark is a great example of how you can get more out of yourself if you really try. Back in the early 1990s he was a typical young guy who liked to go out partying and drinking with his mates. He was not into fitness.

In 1992 I ran in the Brisbane half-marathon and he was at the finish with his cousins to cheer me over the line.

A few days after that event he came to me and said: 'Zia (Italian for Auntie), you have inspired me. I am going to take up jogging too. I'm going to get really fit like you'.

And he did. But he did more. In the mid 1990s when he was in the Russo Institute of Technology marketing team he made the first of several trips to Brazil on a student recruiting drive. When he returned he told our family: 'I'm giving up drinking. The people in Brazil showed me you don't need alcohol to have fun'.

From that day on he never had another drink. He proves his point over and over again with his exuberance and sense of fun by being the life and soul of parties and family gatherings, just drinking water. He really enjoys his life.

He is very successful in his work with us because he generates the kind of positive energy that boosts the enthusiasm and confidence of those around him. Like me, he loves to take business study courses. He attended Cornell University in the US in 2001 and Stanford University in October 2002.

When I look at how far I have come in my business career I marvel at the changes I have seen in the relatively short span of 23 years. In fact, I have seen a complete revolution. My first students used typewriters for writing business documents and they used ledger books for book-keeping. Now those things are gone. The computer has taken over and made everything so much faster, easier and more efficient.

As I reflect on that it seems to me we don't always make the most of changes when they seem too technical and too difficult. I think we've all given the Internet a miss, because of all the dot com failures and the financial woes of the IT world.

But we should open our eyes, because many large companies are now reliant on the Internet as a tool. It is no longer experimental. It's just like driving a motor vehicle to work. You now use the Internet as a vehicle to take you to where it is you want to go or what it is you want to do. For example, a small greengrocer can build up his business, just on the Internet. So it has become like a motor for business, if it's used correctly.

So that is my story, which is still evolving. But I have only skimmed the surface. I have explained what I've done and where I have come from. But more importantly, there is the 'how' and the 'why' of what I have done and what I continue to do.

How do I lead my company, what are my beliefs about leadership, how do I treat my customers, how do I compete, how do I get maximum performance from my staff, how do I communicate, how and why do I network, how do I deal with change, how do I recruit my staff, how do I reward them?

I address those questions – and others – in Part Two of this book, but before we move on to Part Two allow me to review what I have written and reflect on the most important lessons life has taught me.

There are six I would especially like to share. They are:

1. Be loyal to your family and let them into your lives to share your triumphs as well as being there to console you in your time of need. Express your love for them. Their love, their support and their belief in you will give you strength to believe in yourself. I think the young should be grateful if their parents have made them pull their weight, doing their share of jobs around the home and expecting them to earn their pocket money. That's what teaches you a sense of responsibility and accountability and equips you to earn a living later in life. If you get it easy in your teen years, if you get all the spending

money you need without having to work for it, if you get all the Nintendo and PlayStations you want without having to save up for them, my advice is, go out and get a part time job. You have to learn to relate to people in the real world who have to make profits in order to survive and people who have to earn enough wages to support a family. Can you fit into their world? Can you be useful to a business? Can you contribute to a team? You won't find out by staying at home and playing computer games in your bedroom. As I was growing up I thought my father was a tyrant, making us work too hard and taking a large part of our earnings to put into the family fund. When I left home and went into the real world of doing a real day's work for a real day's pay I realised I had reason to be grateful to my father. He gave me my most valuable strengths – the capacity to endure hard work and confidence in myself. All those seemingly impossible things he had given me to do and which I always managed to do, had equipped me to face any challenge with optimism and commitment. He also taught me the value of saving and the basic business skills which have got me where I am today.

2. Never take it personally. Never think, why me? Never accept someone else's negative opinion of you, because it will drain you of your strength. It will fill your mind with self-doubt. Have the positive attitude that whatever they say about you, it's only their opinion. If it's a question about your capacity or your ability, take the attitude that it is you versus your mind. You can do anything if you put your mind to it. It's not what happens to you, it's what you do about it that counts. If you think you can, you're right. If you think you can't, you're also right. When I was the migrant kid ostracised because of the smelly parmesan cheese and salami sandwiches I was taking to school, and also because of my lack of English comprehension, I could have taken it personally, withdrawn into myself and curled up in corners. Know what I did? I hoarded my meagre pocket money, bought a jar of the vegemite everyone else had on their sandwiches and started making my own sandwiches. I even mucked that up by forgetting to put butter on the bread first, but eventually

I got it right and there came that wonderful day when one of the other kids actually swapped sandwiches with me and ate one of mine. I was in! See the lesson here? It wasn't me the kids were rejecting. It was my sandwiches. I had the power to change the sandwiches, so I did. And my English comprehension improved because I worked at it and did not go into a sulk.

3. Associate with positive people and don't let negative people suck you into their world of darkness and doubt. The positive people are those who smile easily and always have a go at things. The negative people are their opposites, those who are glum and believe the world is against them. If you can't find many positive people to associate with, read books written by positive people. Believe me, it works. Let me give you an example. One of the world's greatest motivators is Anthony Robbins, author of several best-selling books including *Unlimited Power* and *Awaken The Giant Within.* He is a valued advisor to the CEOs of Fortune 500 companies, members of two Royal families, former US President Bill Clinton, professional sporting teams and sports stars including Andre Agassi and Greg Norman. But Anthony Robbins had an impoverished, unstable childhood. His parents broke up when he was very young. His mother married twice more and struggled to put food on the table for her son. As a teenager he was frequently beaten up by bigger kids. He had an ego and wouldn't back down to anyone. Anthony turned his mind into a powerful generator of positive energy by reading first one, then hundreds more books on human development, psychology and physiology or, as he says, 'anything about thought'. He recalls that in five years, as a teenager, he read 700 such books. They were the brain food that turned him into the world's great motivator, acclaimed by the International Chamber of Commerce as one of the 10 Outstanding People of the World. His story is another example of using adversity to unleash your determination to rise to a higher level. I had to repeat Grade 4 and failed Grade 10 English at my first try. I also failed Grade 12 senior English twice in evening classes and passed on my third attempt. Giving up was

never on my agenda. Here's a little trick you can use to keep yourself positive. Wear a rubber band around your wrist. When you say something negative like, *I wish I were smarter ... or never make it ... or too hard for me to do* .... just give that rubber band a snap so that it stings your wrist. You can measure the extent of your negativity by the number of red welts you get on your wrist.

4. Be the person you want to be and not the person someone else wants you to be. Be open to help and good advice from others but let no one take you over. My focus was that I had only one life and one journey and I was going to take charge of it without any husband, father or banker controlling my destiny. In my mind it was better to drive my car and pick up my boyfriend than to have him pick me up in his. That's the way I thought. There were young men who wanted to change the way I dressed, the way I spoke and so on, but I was happy being me, and we went our separate ways

5. Use empowering words in your self-talk. Don't underestimate the potency of this. There is scientific evidence that 80 per cent of our day is self-talk. We can choose to negatively talk or positively praise ourselves. It stands to reason that if most of our self-talk is positive, we will act in a positive, *it can be done*, manner. The reverse is true if our thoughts are mostly negative. I have a passionate belief in the power of words to give you strength. In my scrapbook there is a copy of an article written about me several years ago by an interviewer who was fascinated by my tendency to speak in motivational phrases. He was right. I did speak (and think) in such phrases – and I still do – because I attended every motivational seminar that was available to me, and still do as part of the lifetime learning process I have committed myself to. This is an extract of what the interviewer wrote in his article, which was titled *The Rise and Rise of Sarina Russo:* "Sarina Russo likes to speak in those motivational phrases that drip like the sweetest honey from the tongues of entrepreneurs giddy with their own success. Slogans like, *Your attitude determines your altitude* and *the speed of the leader determines*

the speed of the gang. But the remarkable thing about her is that she has found success through living out such phrases, putting flesh on their glibness, giving meaning to words that, for many of us, are without meaning".

6. Never stop learning. The discipline I imposed on myself was to work harder on myself than on my job. I was guided by the message of yet another motivational speaker: *the pain of discipline weighs ounces, the pain of regret weighs tons.* I drew from this the determination to educate myself, to discipline myself with my savings, to find mentors who could inspire me (including my boyfriends), to visit stimulating places, to read good books and listen to uplifting music and to go to as many motivational seminars as I could find about '*how to develop your self esteem and self image*', remembering I never knew the meaning of self-esteem and self image at school. Such a concept was beyond my comprehension.

So where has all of this taken me? The typing class I started in 1979 with nine students has grown into one of the largest and most successful private educational institutions (the Russo Institute of Technology) on the east coast of Australia, catering for students from all over the world in many business disciplines to first year university degree level. An international college – who could believe it? Thousands of students have completed our courses. And we employ a large number of teachers. Our employment agency network, Sarina Russo Job Access, placed tens of thousands of people in jobs in a little over two years.

And it has all come about through the co-operative effort of people who have shared my dream. What I am really most proud of is that I have been able to build up around me such a team of champions.

SARINA RUSSO TIME LINE

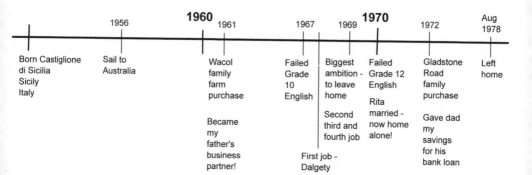

1960   **1970**

1956   1961   1967   1969   1972   Aug 1978

Born Castiglione di Sicilia Sicily Italy

Sail to Australia

Wacol family farm purchase

Became my father's business partner!

Failed Grade 10 English

First job - Dalgety

Biggest ambition - to leave home

Second third and fourth job

Failed Grade 12 English

Rita married - now home alone!

Gladstone Road family purchase

Gave dad my savings for his bank loan

Left home

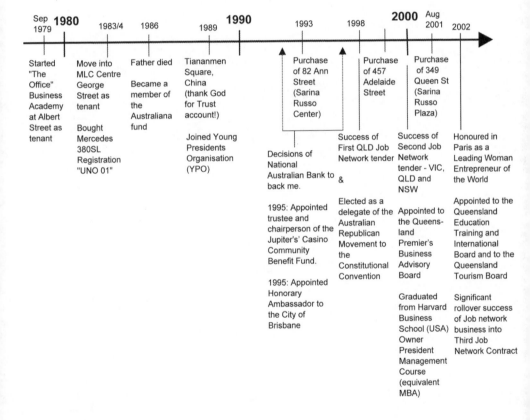

| Sep 1979 | **1980** | 1983/4 | 1986 | 1989 | **1990** | 1993 | 1998 | **2000** | Aug 2001 | 2002 |

Started "The Office" Business Academy at Albert Street as tenant

Move into MLC Centre George Street as tenant

Bought Mercedes 380SL Registration "UNO 01"

Father died

Became a member of the Australiana fund

Tiananmen Square, China (thank God for Trust account!)

Joined Young Presidents Organisation (YPO)

Purchase of 82 Ann Street (Sarina Russo Center)

Decisions of National Australian Bank to back me.

1995: Appointed trustee and chairperson of the Jupiter's Casino Community Benefit Fund.

1995: Appointed Honorary Ambassador to the City of Brisbane

Success of First QLD Job Network tender

&

Elected as a delegate of the Australian Republican Movement to the Constitutional Convention

Purchase of 457 Adelaide Street

Success of Second Job Network tender - VIC, QLD and NSW

Appointed to the Queensland Premier's Business Advisory Board

Graduated from Harvard Business School (USA) Owner President Management Course (equivalent MBA)

Purchase of 349 Queen St (Sarina Russo Plaza)

Honoured in Paris as a Leading Woman Entrepreneur of the World

Appointed to the Queensland Education Training and International Board and to the Queensland Tourism Board

Significant rollover success of Job network business into Third Job Network Contract

Part Two
How to succeed in business

CHAPTER TEN

Learning the art of Leadership

Early in my business career I discovered it wasn't enough to just manage a business. I realised that if I were to grow the business, I had to take myself outside the business and look for inspiration. I didn't know it then, but what I needed to learn was how to be a leader and not just a manager.

There is a theory about business, now a cliché, that goes: You won't take your business anywhere by just working **in** the business. You must also work **on** the business. In other words you need to take a helicopter view of the business. And that is so true. But I took it a step further. I knew I had to work on myself even harder than I worked in, or on, the business.

My life changed when I recognised that for my circumstances to change for the better, I had to make changes to who I was. It would have been easy to say, I can't do this, or I can't do that, because I don't have the skills, or know-how. But I accepted that the skills I had were not adequate to take me to my dream of huge success and financial independence, so I pursued the skills I believed I would need.

I had the feeling that if I could charge the business with enough energy, the business would get bigger, better and more profitable. I knew that the only source the business could get that energy from was me and from recruiting excellent management. Although I had the passion and the desire to succeed I had to learn how to channel it effectively.

But where was I to get this channelling skill from? My background as a migrant kid helped me there. From the age of five I had been the eyes and ears of my father and mother – and older siblings – in adapting from the culture of a small Sicilian village to the big city culture of Brisbane, Australia.

I was a listener and an observer. In business, I decided I had to use those skills to learn how to make my business grow and thrive.

I attended motivational seminars and was excited by the powerful rhetoric that assured me all I had to do to become a huge success was to have a positive attitude and unwavering self-belief.

I was inspired by the message of Jim Rohn, whom I consider to be the doyen of motivational speakers: *'To have more, become more. Work harder on yourself than on your job. The major key to your better future is you'.*

I rubbed shoulders with other people in business at these seminars, listened to their stories and memorised them.

The message I was getting was that anyone can be remarkable. All you had to do was to do ordinary things extraordinarily well, like picking up the telephone in an office with enthusiasm, excitement and interest and making the person at the other end of the line feel special.

I discovered that the more I pushed this message on to the people around me, the more I kept saying to my teaching staff and my students things like, *we can all be champions, we can all be extraordinary, we can all be outstanding,* the more it reflected back on to me and my business. I kept growing and it kept growing.

I took every opportunity to make contact and develop relationships with successful business people through lunches, seminars and business functions.

I networked among them to get jobs for the graduates from my school. I discovered that this networking worked two ways: Not only could I win jobs for my students from those business contacts – they would also refer business to me.

In associating with successful people I began to see the difference between them and the not-so-successful. They were more expansive in their thinking; they seemed to see wider, further and deeper. They were not afraid to honestly express their judgements of anything that was sub-standard and they seemed to have vision.

What I was being exposed to in these people was something I was not able to put a name to until years later: it was leadership as opposed to management. They led. They paid others to manage.

Let me explain the difference, as I see it, between a manager and a leader.

By definition, a leader is an individual who is going somewhere, heading to, or pointing to, new horizons. Leaders have visionary qualities that draw others along with them toward a declared destination or goal. They may lead from in front – or, as shepherds, they may guide from behind.

Managers are not necessarily going anywhere. Their job is to stay put and manage what is around them.

Some people say you cannot learn leadership. I disagree. If you open your ears, your eyes and your mind, and have a belief in yourself, you can learn ... as I did.

Leadership is not a gift that is flashed down to you by some cosmic force, nor do I believe you are born with it. Leadership is a skill that comes from experience and if you are managing the experience well, the rewards will flow.

By managing it well I mean you should not just be making money; you should also be monitoring your own performance. Are you going about things in the most appropriate way? Have you found a way to inspire the people who work for you so that your business is in a process of continuous improvement?

To answer those questions you must constantly be learning how leaders who are really successful behave. You have to make yourself a student of success, a scholar of good ideas. You must look for benchmarks and role models.

That's exactly what I have done. Over the years I could have bought a house with the amount I have spent on self-education and developing relationships with people who can help me to grow.

I have been lucky. I have studied in the world's most advanced business education programs, and that has been an advantage, but even if those programs are not open to you, the principle is the same: learning is the key to your personal development as a leader. Seek out courses and programs that are within your reach and take them.

As I wrote in Chapter Four, 10 years after I opened my typing school my business had grown to such an extent that I was invited, at the age of 38, to become a member of the Young Presidents' Organisation (YPO). It was a great honour to be invited – and to be the first Queensland woman to have been invited – to join this select group. But most of all it was an incredible learning experience. Thank you, YPO, I will be indebted to you for the rest of my life.

As I also wrote in Chapter Four I wasn't certain that I could justify spending the money required to attend an Owner President Management Course at Harvard, but did so after another YPO member, a woman, who was the CEO of a New York company many times bigger than mine, said to me: 'Sarina, do it. Once you graduate out of this course, you will take your company to another level'.

I did it and, after graduating from it, my company won a major contract that led to massive growth in our operations. Never in my wildest dreams had I imagined such a thing would happen to me. But what carried me through the challenges of that contract process was the charge of confidence I got from having done that Harvard course. I had enough belief in my ability to feel that I and the people of my company could take on any challenge. That belief came from my learning experience at Harvard.

I said to my YPO friend: 'You were right. It's happened. We have taken our business to a higher level. Thank you'.

Imagine how much my leadership style has had to change since 1979 when I had just nine students and a part time staff of two, whereas today hundreds of people work in the Sarina Russo Group of companies and we teach thousands of students every year and fill tens of thousands of vacancies in the recruitment market.

Back then I saw leadership as a workday function, a job. Today it is a way of life. I have discovered that I have to live the role of leader. It is now a 24-hour job.

The first rule of leadership

Over the years, as I have put myself through a process of continuous learning, studying others in the Harvard environment to see how they lead and also learn, I kept asking myself, what sort of person do I have to become to carry this massive responsibility as a CEO?

I came to this conclusion: number one, you have to be a leader who shows certainty. We're living in a globalised environment, a world that is constantly changing. I see it as my responsibility as the CEO to make sure that all the uncertainty that surrounds us in the wider world is contained and managed by certainty within my organisation.

As a CEO, even though you may have self-doubt, you must use your emotional intelligence and portray confidence in your voice and power in your language and your message. You must create that certainty.

Because if you don't show that, you are not going to have respect from your team, from your management.

They are going to start doubting you. So it's very, very important that, even though you may have that self-doubt (am I doing the right thing?) it's better to make a decision than no decision. You are respected a lot more in management if you make some changes rather than allowing situations to keep festering. You may be afraid to terminate a certain manager. He or she may be great to have dinner with, a moral person and very intelligent, but if they are hopelessly under-performing you have to do something about it. Not just for the sake of your business, but for the sake of the people in the organisation who may suffer through your inaction.

So I have a policy of always speaking the truth. If I cannot speak the truth to my people, I can never expect them to change. For example, I may deal with one of my teams by saying, 'how do you think you guys are going?'.

Some of them may say, 'we're doing well'.

If that's not my belief, I will say, 'let me tell you the truth'. Then I will speak the truth and I will tell them exactly what is happening. I will ask them what they think they can do to make a change to their performance.

Then I'll leave them with solutions. I'll leave them with an understanding of the truth – that there is so much more that has to be done if they are to achieve the performance we require.

If they have indeed been doing well, I will speak the truth about that, too. I will spell out how well they have been doing and I will congratulate them for it. If it has been a turnaround from poor results to excellent results I will celebrate it with them.

What it's all about is honesty. When people know that you tell the truth about all things, that you are always honest, they trust you. The most important thing about that is that when they trust you, they believe what you say – and then they will do what you request, suggest or command. And that is the most valuable power a leader can have.

Where there is distrust, there is no belief. Your words are treated with suspicion and cynicism. Therefore, you have no power. And that brings me to a most important point. You do not **take** power. You cannot **assume** power. You must **earn** it through your words and your actions. It must be given to you by those you lead – and it will not be given to you unless your followers, your people, trust you in what you say and what you do.

So the simple equation is: truth in all things, honesty in all things, produces trust and trust produces power and influence.

Truth, honesty and trust. These to me are the three most important qualities to instil into a business. In any company you've got to understand that you are creating security for yourselves. You're also creating security for the team. And you're also creating security for your customers. When you have truth, honesty and trust, you have the power to create an awareness that it's everybody's responsibility to make sure they really do perform.

My team know how I feel, not what they want to hear. They have a choice to either come with me to a higher level or be left behind. So leadership to me is one of certainty, because we live in an uncertain world.

I constantly exhort myself and my staff to, *think like a customer ... or staple yourself to an order.* To me, that says it all. There really is no business unless you sell something.

In a service industry business like mine, everyone in the organisation must be a seller of something, even if it is no more than a welcoming smile (and it must be brilliant). Knowing your customer, understanding your customer and most of all, understanding your customer's options, are essential if you are to keep that customer and win others.

My 20 rules of leadership

To live the role of leader, to be _seen_ to be the leader, I follow a set of 20 rules that govern my attitude and my behaviour.

Rule Number One: I live each day with three objectives constantly in my mind:

(1) To make sure there's direction; (2) to make sure there's certainty; and (3) to foster a feeling of _there's something in it for me_ throughout the organisation, whether you are an area manager or an employee.

One of the things I drive is that the organisation is only an instrument to its management and its employees in enabling them to achieve what they want to achieve. They've got to work out what they want to have through the organisation, what they want to see through the organisation, what they want to become, and what they want to do.

The organisation is purely a vehicle for their personal and professional needs. When you have that attitude, individuals feel empowered that they too can get something out of this company called ours. To me, it's very, very important that I have that culture.

If you can't maximise the power of the individual in your company, you haven't done anything. If you expand the ability of individuals in your organisation, you expand the ability of the whole organisation. Grasping that concept has helped me as a leader to expand and develop my business enormously and I have taken my management team with me.

Rule Number Two: The leader must determine urgency and speed. I think the speed of the leader determines the speed of the gang. Once a leader shows some complacency, the complacency immediately is transmitted to your management team and through the culture of your managers to your individual employees.

It's extremely important that even if you feel a little complacent, you never show it. If you do, you're better off going on holiday or taking yourself elsewhere for the day.

Never come into an organisation like mine and show that you are going through some complacency or some compromise because the leader must communicate the standards.

Those standards must be your vision and your values. The leader's responsibility is to build a vision and it's up to the management to execute that vision and then to filter it through down the chain.

Rule Number Three: Be the image-maker. Develop a presence. To be a leader you should look like a leader in your dress and in your demeanour through the working day. Remember you are the brand, you are the example to follow. It's important that you take care of your appearance and come in looking successful and feeling successful. Branding is a crucially important element in my business, as in any business. As the leader, I am part of that branding. My image is reflected on the rest of my team. When I walk in every morning it's absolutely critical that I look professional and that I carry that professionalism through everything I do, down to the way I leave my desk in the evening. I could leave my office with files on the floor, files on the table, but I don't. I'll always clean up so that the next morning my desk is neat and tidy, ready for the start of the day.

Rule Number Four: Be a clear and strong communicator. Once every week I send out an email to all my staff, titled, *from Sarina's desk*, and I tell them about some activity or event I have been involved in. I like them all to know what's happening, why it's happening and what it means to the business. I welcome any comments. I empower all of my staff to feel part of a family culture by following the principle that nobody cares how much you know until they know how much you care. I have regular meetings with my management and my financial people, at which I speak my truth to them and they speak theirs to me.

Here is an example of what I write in my emails to everyone in the Sarina Russo Group of companies. This one was written to mark the beginning of the year 2002.

From:	Sarina Russo
Sent:	Monday, January 14, 2002 10:53
To:	SRJA All Staff; RIT All Staff
Subject:	from Sarina's desk....Happy New Year
Importance:	High

Hi Guys,

Well, the Christmas festive season is truly over as we pack our Christmas tree and decorations one more time and put them in storage ... so now to our big year of 2002...

I have had a wonderful break ... For the first time I truly committed myself to relax and have time out and now it's time to rev up! I am travelling to Boston again this year and will truly look forward to my Harvard Educational Experience. I will tell you more during the end of the week about my plans!

I would like to share with you my resolutions regarding my professional life and one of the biggest resolutions for me is to be the best CEO ever! To be able to communicate with all of you guys and to empower each one of you to maximise your capacity in performance and in your professional careers with our Organisation. This of course requires discipline and determination to give of your best. It's really simple. That is, feel good about yourself and excel in everything you do! Of course your health and fitness is paramount to achieving excellent results. I think in my time at the Gold Coast (I was down there for one week) I power-walked 60 kilometres. I felt so good about my efforts!

Well, yes, challenges for 2002 will be inevitable. My prediction this year is that if we all excel at an urgent pace we will take this Group of Companies to an incredible level and secure our positions both professionally and financially!

So from me to you I hope that 2002 brings you and your families and friends all that you wish for. Remember to set small and large goals and reflect on what you have achieved in the past. Remember, with your determination you can achieve a lot more...Let's go team. I am truly refreshed and ready to give it my very very best shot. Are you all ready>>>>>>Let's go!

Happy New Year once again and congratulations to all those people and teams who won such excellent awards at the Christmas Awards night. What a euphoric night we all had. I think there were a few headaches the following morning or maybe we were just on an absolute high.

I will see you at the top and look forward to personally supporting you all. And remember my philosophy is that I am here for you, so you can email me, write, phone or personally contact me.

Have a Great Year ... and let's make this the best year ever in our lives! ... IT CAN BE DONE! From...

Sarina ... Your Happy and invigorated CEO... Happy New Year!!

Rule Number Five: Safeguard your health and fitness. As a leader, you have to find a way to give yourself some relief from the many unavoidable stresses that are part and parcel of the pressure cooker world we live in and the weight you carry in being a leader.

I find the only way for me to release my stress is in some form of exercise. You've got to have a fit body and if you have a fit body, you have a fit mind.

I have what I call my daily 'one hour boardroom retreat' which is me in a fitness environment, whether it's in the pool or running around the track or doing something that's physically strenuous.

Those physical activity sessions are a form of mobile meditation and they help me lower my stress level. I recommend regular massage.

Rule Number Six: Stay level-headed in difficult situations. As a leader you cannot, must not, transfer your stress to others. I think it's important that when you walk into your organisation each day there's some calmness about you as well.

Rule Number Seven: Spread the load and delegate. If you're feeling challenged, I think it's really important to share that challenge with your management team and ask for help. For example, say *I need you to help me with this challenge. What do you think we should do?'.* And empower people. Let them contribute. Listen to them. Even if you don't agree, give them the ability to feel that their contribution is of added value.

Rule Number Eight: Keep looking and listening to the 'buzz' of your business so that you are constantly monitoring its health. A good leader should know his or her business as well as a doctor would know what a patient's vital signs should be. Imprint the anatomy of your business into your brain. Every part of the business body should be healthy. It's crucially important to recognise it if some part of your business is dying. You may have to cut off an arm so that it doesn't disease the rest of the body. Don't shirk that decision.

Rule Number Nine: Don't fight change. Use it. It's important that you understand that business changes, that the needs of people, the consumers, vary and people want more or want to be inspired and stimulated by your environment. See change as an opportunity for your business to do more **for** your customers in order to get more **from** your customers. You've got to be able to embrace change rather than regard it with fear and trepidation. You've got to embrace it with passion and excitement and take your team along and make it a window of opportunity of whatever it is that you need to be challenged with. Think about this phrase: massive change makes stability exciting.

Rule Number Ten: Reward performance unstintingly. Provide an incentive scheme or profit sharing so that your people find there is room for them to make money and secure themselves financially. Acknowledge and recognise individual performances with warm and enthusiastic praise.

Rule Number Eleven: Celebrate your progress. I believe in putting on the biggest Christmas party, taking my people to a ball room, with the silver service and the five star treatment and I don't spare the cost. A lot of people around Christmas never get this sort of exposure. It's a great boost for them to feel that the boss really values them and also wants them to share the success of the year that has passed.

I also believe in regular social functions. We have a regular barbe-cue/drinks night on our rooftop recreation area where staff can let their hair down with food and drinks, looking out over the lights of the city. There is a relaxed and fun-charged atmosphere at this function that sets thoughts flowing and ideas bubbling. It promotes friendliness and bonding. Your people benefit and your business benefits. A happy business is a successful business.

Rule Number Twelve: Build relationships. As a CEO you must network with your staff. When you are in a service industry, as I am, your inventory is your staff. You must know them by name and understand what they do – and be available to them. I have an open door policy, so that anyone can email me, phone me, write to me, walk into my office. Regardless of whether they're people at the front line or management I believe it is important for them to know they have that opportunity to talk to me and tell me their feelings. I like to do boardroom lunches and get to know them. People will extract information from me, and vice versa, on things that would never be shared if you were behind a desk.

Rule Number Thirteen: Don't age-group yourself. Interact with young people and be '*with it*' by immersing yourself in events that excite you and stimulate you and by surrounding yourself with people who are 'groovy'. A whole different, happening world is going on out there via cyber land and it is the young who are tapped into it. Connect with them and stay tuned for new opportunities, personally and professionally.

Rule Number Fourteen: Be good to yourself, reward yourself. I think it's important that you come home to a place you like. For all of your efforts and commitment, treat yourself with special things to keep you motivated. In my case that translates to a beautiful home and a great lifestyle.

Rule Number Fifteen: Be smart about banking. Develop a relationship with your Bank Manager beyond the phone call and the business meeting. Do lunches or do dinners. Always have a second bank on a string, because one may go along with you for a while and then have a change of policy that cuts you out. It's best to borrow money when you don't need it because it's always easier to get – and you get it on better terms when you're not desperate.

Rule Number Sixteen: Look for milestones to mark your achievements. Let them be monuments to your efforts. The greatest thing for me was buying my first high-rise building because it put us on the map and marked our success in creating the Russo Institute of Technology.

Rule Number Seventeen: It's really important to have a balanced life, which means having interests and friendships outside the business. I have some wonderful friends around the world with whom I am in constant contact. I have my Mum who's my emotional stability. Then I have my family, my nieces and nephews and my sisters and my brother. It's very, very important to share and let them share your success as well.

Rule Number Eighteen: Take joy in continuing to lead in a direction where everyone's going to gain – not only your customers but also your internal people. If you don't grow your business, parts of your business anatomy will wither and die.

Looking back over 23 years, my business has seen nothing but growth and through it I have achieved economies of scale. It's like a plane that flies to a timetable. No matter how many bookings, the plane has still got to fly. Obviously it's better to have it full, so airlines invent all kinds of discounted fare structures to get planeloads of people, even though many will have paid different fares.

It's the same in my industry. It's much more profitable to have a big lecture room filled with students than to have only 10 sitting there. Growth in the education environment gives you the opportunity to do more research, achieve more development, create more excitement, open up more international opportunities and develop more vision for 21st century business growth.

Sarina with Senior Harvard Business School Lecturer Ben Shapiro.

Sarina with good friend Fiona Snedden, daughter of the late Sir Billy Snedden.

Sarina with graduates at the Russo Institute of Technology. Former Dean of the Institute, John Slater is at left.

Sarina with President Bill Clinton at a Sydney function.

Bill Clinton speaks to a forum of business leaders including
Sarina Russo (second left) in a closed session in New Zealand, 2002.

Sarina (right) with Harvard Business School classmates at a fun party night in Boston.

Sarina in class at the Harvard Business School.

Sarina lunching with nephew Marcello Pennisi in the Windows on the World Restaurant on the 106th floor of the North Tower of the World Trade Centre, New York, in 1998.

Sarina completing a 10km fun run in Brisbane 1999.

Sarina took this snap of Sir Paul McCartney and his new bride Heather Mills when she met them on the stairs at the Wimbledon Tennis finals in 2002. She gave Sir Paul a kiss on the cheek.

Sarina compares notes with a man she calls her 'entrepreneurial hero', Virgin supremo Sir Richard Branson, at a Media Ball in Parliament House, Brisbane.

Sarina with sisters Rosina (left) and Rita at a Christmas celebration.

Sarina with Michael Barnes, General Manager of the Russo Institute of Technology.

Sarina with NSW Premier Bob Carr after a Sydney function in March 2002.

Sarina enjoys a night out partying with her relatives in Castiglione during a visit to Sicily in 2001.

*With Marcello Pennisi, niece Angela Berlese and nephew Mark Berlese
during the visit to Castiglione in 2001.*

Sarina enjoys an outing with friends Janina Cowley (left)
and Lynne Pask on a sunny Brisbane afternoon.

Sarina with Prime Minister John Howard on Budget night 2002.

Now growth can also be painful unless you embrace the challenges that go with it. What happens is that the dynamics of the company changes. Management expands, and some executives will feel insecure because of the structural change, while others feel very empowered as a result.

What you need to do, as a good leader, is to understand what growth is doing to the key people inside your business so that you are able to ensure that everyone is still driven by growth.

Rule Number Nineteen: Don't let you or your staff run out of challenges. And unless you grow, that is exactly what will at happen. When it does, your unchallenged staff will then look at your competitors who are growing and go to them because there is a more exciting challenge there. I believe in developing our people and growing entrepreneurs within.

Rule Number Twenty: Look beyond the immediate horizon. Constantly challenge yourself in expanding your skills. For me, this meant looking beyond my home state of Queensland into the southern states of NSW and Victoria and also overseas.

I used to lack confidence at the thought of expanding my business down south. How could I manage it from Queensland? But once I was given that opportunity through our Job Network business contract, I embraced the challenge.

By deciding to bite the bullet and move beyond our local boundaries I created for myself a challenge to do more, to offer more and to increase awareness in the consumer market of our products and services. And now we can also do it globally.

If you don't grow your business, ultimately what you are offering can become redundant or superfluous. By having diverse products and services, you can secure your investment – and your staff and consumers. That is my focus.

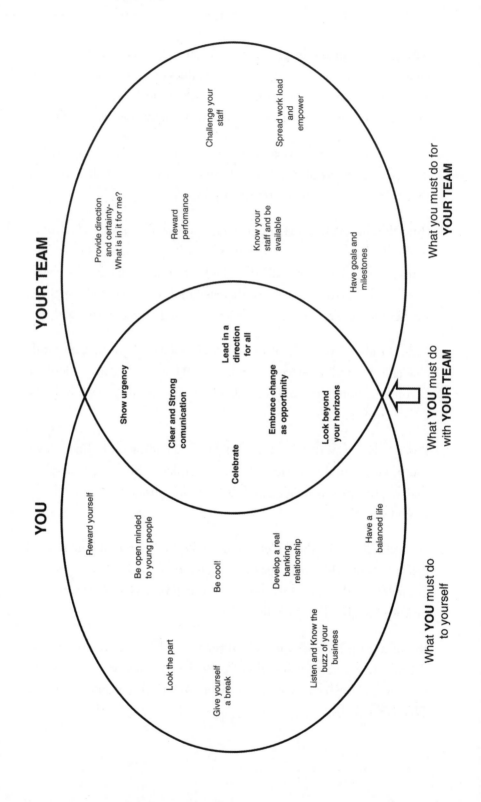

RUSSO LEADERSHIP RULES

YOU

YOUR TEAM

What YOU must do to yourself

What YOU must do with YOUR TEAM

What you must do for YOUR TEAM

Reward yourself

Be open minded to young people

Be cool!

Develop a real banking relationship

Have a balanced life

Look the part

Give yourself a break

Listen and Know the buzz of your business

Show urgency

Clear and Strong comunication

Celebrate

Lead in a direction for all

Embrace change as opportunity

Look beyond your horizons

Provide direction and certainty-What is in it for me?

Reward perfomance

Know your staff and be available

Have goals and milestones

Challenge your staff

Spread work load and empower

CHAPTER ELEVEN

The importance of corporate ethics

Events in the US and Australia in the past couple of years have tested public confidence in the ethics of big business. The collapses of companies like Enron and WorldCom in the US and HIH and OneTel in Australia have painted a picture of greed and reckless extravagance at the highest levels.

In the wake of the corporate scandals in the US there is now a requirement that chief executives and their chief financial officers separately certify any financial reports and be liable for their veracity. In other words, the CEO has to personally endorse a financial report as being true and correct and to accept liability if it turns out not to be true and correct. Huge fines and imprisonment could be the consequence of signing off on a false and misleading report.

I agree with that requirement. I insist on my business being completely ethical in all respects. I pride myself on being a happy taxpayer. I don't want to rort tax systems or any systems, I don't want to take advantage of any customer. We will always go the extra mile in training or in providing any other service to ensure that our customers are satisfied they have received value for what they have been charged.

I believe CEOs have to take the lead in the integrity stakes. The CEO has to _believe_ that being ethical in all things and being _seen_ to be ethical in all things, is the only way to go. The CEO has to imprint ethical practices into the culture of the company or organisation and to act swiftly to stamp out any dubious or unethical practices anywhere down the line in the business.

Loss of business and diving profits could be the consequence of not having that culture in place. Wrong-doing at the top could destroy the brand of your business. Even the suspicion of wrong-doing by the CEO of a company can do serious damage to that company's business.

We're seeing that happen right now as I write this book. For many years Martha Stewart was an icon of virtue in the American business community. She also happened to be a role model of mine – and we met in a hairdressing salon in Manhattan, New York in June 2002.

As a young woman she had a successful modelling career, then had a child and began a second successful career as a stockbroker. When recession hit Wall Street in 1973 she left stockbroking and moved to Westport, Connecticut and restored an 1805 farmhouse. She started a catering business from home in 1972.

In 10 years this business became a $1 billion enterprise called Martha Stewart Living Omnimedia Inc. She had her own magazine, Martha Stewart Living, with a circulation of more than 2 million, her own TV shows, Martha Stewart Living and Martha's Kitchen, a book publishing business, a merchandising business and a mail order catalogue business, Martha by Mail.

She had an Internet sales business that had more than 1 million registered users. Sales of Martha Stewart branded homeware products through the Kmart chain in the US totalled around $1 billion every year. Through her media activities she reached 88 million people a month.

Her amazing success began with a single book she published in 1982. It was titled, *Entertaining*, based on her experience in her home-based catering business. She came to be described as the Queen of Catering, the Doyenne of Decorating and the Empress of the US Lifestyle Industry. In American eyes she could do no wrong.

But in June 2002 her brand turned sour and America turned off their Queen of Catering. Why? Because it was revealed she was being investigated for insider trading. Nothing was proved and nothing was admitted, but she and her company were besmirched by the allegations and the innuendos contained in the blaze of media attention she received. It was no longer chic to buy anything branded Martha Stewart.

And it got worse. In August 2002 she was sued by shareholderers in her company because they alleged that by her actions she caused a dive in the value of their shareholding. And it got worse still. It was alleged she had engaged in insider trading not once but twice. And what made it all seem even worse still was that she was a member of the Stock Exchange (but has since resigned).

Shares in her company plunged from more than $20 a share to less than $10, chopping more than $130 million off her personal assets.

Her world began to fall apart when it was announced that a Congressional Committee was probing why she sold shares in a company named Imclone a day ahead of a Food and Drug Administration decision to reject a new cancer drug developed by Imclone called Erbitux.

The Imclone shares nose-dived from a high of $84 per share after the FDA rejection. Martha Stewart admitted she sold 4000 Imclone shares ahead of the news of that rejection, not because she had inside information but because she had a standing stop-loss order with her broker to sell them if they dropped below $60, which they had done.

But investigators were pressing ahead with their probe into the allegation that Martha Stewart had been tipped off by the former CEO of Imclone about the FDA rejection before it was announced. The Imclone CEO, said to be a friend of Martha Stewart's, was arrested and charged with securities fraud, conspiracy and perjury over allegations that he had organised a sell-off of his company's shares ahead of the announcement of the FDA rejection.

For Martha Stewart it was guilt by association. But then it got personal. In August 2002 it was alleged that she and a group of associates had sold about 5.3 million shares in her own company ahead of the news that she was being investigated over the sale of her shares in the Imclone stock.

It was alleged she and her associates made more than $79 million in illegal profits and avoided losses they would have suffered if the public had known in advance about investigations into Stewart's sale of the Imclone stock.

As I write this, the case is still going on, without resolution and Martha Stewart has found it necessary to resign her membership of the Stock Exchange. To me, it is all a terrible shame. In the way she started her business and grew it, she was a wonderful example to us all. But I repeat, when you lead a company, particularly a public company trading on the stock exchange, you must be seen to be above reproach.

When you are a leader of a company, public or private, you are in a position of trust. To knowingly engage in any activity that is unethical or illegal or to put yourself in a position of being suspected of engaging in any activity that is unethical or illegal, is a betrayal of the trust that your employees, your financial backers, your supppliers and your customers have held in you.

In Martha Stewart's case she had been seen by masses of women across America, over many years, to be their paragon of virtue, someone they admired, respected and looked up to. Imagine the shock when her integrity and ethics were put into question. Could they believe this woman any more, follow her advice any more?

And she had not even been convicted of any wrong-doing.

But she is the brand of the business. She had been sullied by suspicion so the brand was sullied along with her.

What lies ahead? There are two questions. Can the business survive without her if she chooses to walk away into retreat from the public eye? And can it survive with her if she chooses to stay and remains under a cloud of suspicion?

I'm not sure what the answer is on either count, but I would have to say I don't like her chances.

There is a bottom line here. Your brand, your image is everything. Look after your brand and your brand will look after you. To put it at risk to achieve some short-term gain is not only foolish, but self destructive.

Without your integrity and your self-respect you have nothing.

Paul Wilson, a Brisbane writer and criminologist, wrote an article in the Brisbane Courier Mail reflecting on the state of corporate governance around the world. What he said reflected my beliefs perfectly.

He asked: 'Why do so many company CEOs and directors, regardless of background, commit what are at best unethical and at worst criminal actions...? Fortunately there are a lot of honest and ethical CEOs and directors controlling billion-dollar companies who also have the opportunity to rip off their shareholders, employees and the public at large. Instead, they build great business enterprises that serve society well.

'Those who study white collar offenders suggest that the worst criminals share certain characteristics. They are extremely ambitious, ruthless and utterly confident about the correctness of their options and actions.

'Most entrepreneurs are risk-takers, but the worst corporate crooks do not care who they hurt in the process of taking risks. Their endgame is to win the deal and accumulate as much money for themselves as they can'.

Wilson observed that a study by the American Coalition Against Insurance Fraud showed that the public largely tolerates financial crime as demonstrated by their attitude to insurance scams. Nearly two thirds of those surveyed tolerated scams against insurance companies and believed that when frauds occurred, the company deserved to be the target. Only a third of those surveyed considered there were no excuses.

He noted that in appealing to American CEOs to clean up their act, Federal Reserve Chairman Alan Greenspan urged them to adopt ethical and moral standards.

He wrote: 'He is right, of course. Perhaps, though, in the light of the insurance fraud survey, he should also have asked ordinary people to clean up their act as well'.

CHAPTER TWELVE

Recruiting the right people

To me, the question of recruiting people to work in my business is as simple as this: to be the best in my industry, I have to hire the best. So I keep the hiring process simple and focused. The people who are needed to fill vacancies anywhere in my business are recruited by the managers they will be working with, because they know better than any personnel specialist could hope to know what the job requires and what kind of personality will fit.

But there is a proviso. I get the final say. Yes, I am totally hands-on in the hiring department. My managers will produce a short list of their preferred candidates and I will do the final interview and make the selection.

In our Job Access business we have a low management turnover and when vacancies do arise, we often do not have to advertise because our managers have lists of people within the industry who have indicated they would like to join us.

Why? Because they know we offer careers, not just jobs and that we are successful in what we do. We grow entrepreneurs. We have a policy of promoting from within, wherever possible. It's the old story. Success breeds success.

I always say to my managers: *Is the person you are going to refer to me for a final interview an A-plus?* And they know what an A-plus is by my definition.

An A-plus is someone with attitude, someone who has got a good sense of energy and urgency, someone who has got good grooming, who is personable, who has got the skills, who has got the potential to be great, who is out there to want more in his or her life, because if you want more in your life, you'll want more for others.

The other thing is they must be the kind of people who are going to fit in. And I really believe in recruiting local knowledge. It's always good to get local people for local sales in your offices unless you are looking for an eye specialist. You might have to recruit all over the world for that particular skill, but if it's a skill that is common and you can find it in your own community, my advice is to recruit local people for local jobs.

What you'll find is that people can relate, your customers can relate better with staff who are of their own environment.

When you're recruiting, you've got to look at your payroll and make sure that the productivity level from the people you hire is going to give you that return with a significant margin, otherwise you are going to have enormous challenges in your business.

You must know what is your total wages to total sales percentage and set a benchmark so that the numbers leave you with a profit.

So if you invest a large part of your revenue in people, doesn't it make sense to have the best? To make sure that people are productive, that there are key performance indicators, that they are challenged, that they have responsibility and accountability, that they must perform, or else?

For your own survival, you must get your return on investment in your people. That is paramount.

When we won the big Job Network contract, one of my biggest priorities, biggest challenges, was to interview every job candidate. I was determined to have only the best people on my team – my inventory.

I recruited almost 200 people and I made sure they were our culture, that I could work with them, that they had the same values as us, they had the same speed of urgency as we did, that they wanted the opportunity to grow and develop, to be challenged, and they wanted to be part of our organisation on a long-term basis.

The most important quality, I think, is attitude. You can have all the skills in the world but if you don't have a positive attitude, there's no growth for an individual.

Another factor that is really important to me, as a general rule, is whether people are fit. If they are lazy people and have no discipline in their health, let me tell you, it's going to transmit into their performance.

So I encourage fitness. I want people who are interested in being alert in mind, being refreshed by exercise.

I also try to find people who can relate to my work ethics and values. Of course, I realise we can't have everyone like me because that would become a fiery environment. I recognise that I must also have people who have strengths I do not have and people who complement my style and I seek them out as well.

I like to be sure that the people we recruit have got the potential to want to be more. One of the things I say to my staff is *accept who you are today, in pursuit of what you want to be tomorrow ... I want you, too, to have personal goals and to understand that the organisation is the vehicle to what it is you want to do on a personal level like, for example, purchasing your own home, or a block of land.*

To me, this is the essence of powering up your staff to make your business hum with energy, drive, achievement and purpose. Having people working their hardest for you because they believe there is something in it of real value for them is the best defence against what I call the cycle of mediocrity because it promotes an environment in which you have high employee satisfaction and low employee turnover.

So what is the cycle of mediocrity? It's simply this: when there is low employee job satisfaction and high staff turnover, a business falls into a downward spiral that causes sales and profits to plummet.

Low employee job satisfaction leads to a poor service attitude which in turn leads to low customer satisfaction.

High employee turnover with its constant parade of new faces disrupts continuity with customers who look elsewhere for constancy and reliability. This, of course, means a fall in profits and as profits fall there is less money to train staff and to reward them. So the cycle of mediocrity perpetuates.

Of all the lessons I learned at the Harvard Business School, that is probably the most important. Your staff are your drive, your energy, your most valuable asset. You have to know how to choose them well, how to switch them on and keep them switched on.

Studies by Harvard researchers have suggested that employees place a high value in their jobs on capability, which translates as the latitude and ability to deliver results to both internal and external customers. In other words they value being set free to do their job in the best possible way without interference and excessive administration. They value ownership of the process.

High perceived capability, the researchers say, can lead to reductions in the rate of employee turnover.

Knowing the cost of making poor recruitment decisions puts more urgency on getting the recruitment equation right. By hiring the wrong people you are going to incur additional recruiting and training expenses and you will suffer lower productivity from co-workers and managers.

Those are visible costs. However, there are also hidden costs arising from a deterioration in the morale of other employees, from a lowering of the quality of service your business provides and from a loss of customers.

The way to avoid the cycle of mediocrity is to take the approach I take – and that is to put priority on attitude when you recruit staff. Put attitude first and skills second. Skills can be taught, but attitude is a different kettle of fish. You first have to demolish an existing attitude to supplant it with a new one. And that's extremely difficult because it calls for demolition of a mindset and beliefs that have been built up over a lifetime.

Before I hire anyone I need to be satisfied that they will have a customer-focused attitude. I don't want anyone in our organisation who does not have that attitude. No matter where they will be in the organisation they should still have it.

Remember, we all have customers to serve, no matter what we do, even if we're not in the front line of service. If there is no customer for what you do in an organisation, then why are you there?

Take software programmers in a backroom product development role in a business. They may never see an external customer. But they do have customers – the co-workers who will be using, or selling, the software they produce.

Consider the situation if those programmers were so fussy and egotistical that they wouldn't meet deadlines for the release of their software programmes to their co-workers, leaving their co-workers (their customers) with no product to work on.

If the attitude of those programmers is not corrected, delays will continue and the most highly skilled of their down-the-line co-workers will be driven by frustration to find jobs with a competitor, simply because the programmers put themselves before their customers.

So, rule No. 1 is: everyone must have a customer-focused attitude. You can't have pockets of negative, self-serving attitudes.

My rule No. 2 is: all new employees must receive training in the skills and tools they need to perform their jobs well. I don't mean training only in technical skills. I also believe in coaching in interpersonal skills for people in all levels of the organisation. Constant coaching like, 'do you answer the phone with a smile in your voice?'.

I believe in this catchcry: *repetition is the mother of skill. If you keep hearing something over and over again you can only become a master yourself. So make sure the message is always positive and upbeat.*

Again following the principle that we all have customers, I believe coaching in people skills is just as important for the 'back office' people as it is for those who will be spending most of their time serving external customers.

How can you have effective, successful teamwork if you let people into the organisation who don't know how to get on with their fellow workers? What I am talking about is making a can-do, positive, attitude the core of your culture.

I want an office that is full of smiles and has an atmosphere of fun. People who have fun in their work will always achieve more than those who get no fun out of what they do.

The kind of management model I encourage is one based on working with others through who you are, working through a much greater sense of yourself and how you are with other people rather than formal authority.

I believe I am able to succeed in this for two reasons. The first is because I have learned how to pick the right people. I have a sense of who has the personality that will be able to work through professional relationships rather than formal authority.

The second is that a high proportion of the people who work for us have the emotional intelligence to be able to work with others through who they are.

My objective is to recruit winners, and my policy is to do everything I can to help them become winners in the positions they hold in our organisation, so I make sure I provide them with the tools and support they need to perform better and feel better in their jobs.

It comes down to this: selecting the right people, training them to make sure they have the right skills, giving them effective support and the freedom to deliver value to customers.

One of our Job Search Trainers in Queensland achieved the best results of any job search trainer in any organisation in Australia. She was asked by a journalist why she had been so successful. In our organisation, she said, she was inspired by the freedom she was given to make decisions on her own and to act as she saw fit. She was also motivated by the knowledge that the results she was achieving were being noticed. She knew that the reports she wrote were percolating right to the top of the organisation, because I would call her to talk to her about them and to congratulate her on her results.

She felt good about that because it made her feel that her work really mattered and that she mattered. She really enjoyed working with the people she was training because of the positive difference it was making to their lives.

She demonstrates this belief of mine: your staff must have the power and the responsibility to make decisions and to recover quickly from mistakes.

And the force that gives them that power and responsibility must be you, the leader. You must:

1. Establish a sense of urgency;

2. Develop a vision and strategy;

3. Communicate the range of that vision. Spell it out;

4. Empower your people. They'll throw obstacles at you but get rid of the obstacles;

5. Encourage risk-taking, to go out there and nail down that client. The worst they can say is no;

6. Generate short-term wins. It's just great to win a bit;

7. Consolidate gain and produce more change. Continuously do a little more change, because a lot of people are intimidated by change. They find it scary. We have to educate our people to embrace change with passion and excitement; and

8. Understand the Internet. It's really changed our speed. It's given us the opportunity to be more effective, productive and globally competitive.

CHAPTER THIRTEEN

Managing performance

Hire only the best people and naturally you will get high level performance throughout your organisation. Well, it's true that good people will usually find a way to achieve good results for themselves, but it does not necessarily follow that a set of good individual results will represent the collective, or corporate, result your business needs for success.

There needs to be a structure and a strategy that makes it possible for all of your people not just to do their best, but to excel, not only in the interests of your business but in their own interests as well. The trick is to make those interests dovetail.

You can't force people to excel. They must want to excel. And you, as the employer, must create a climate of excelling, or, more properly, excellence.

To create that climate you, the leader, must 'sell' a vision to your people of the direction in which you want to go and the objectives you want to achieve. You must lead by example – the speed of the leader determines the speed of the team. You must motivate and empower staff to achieve their personal best and encourage initiative and creativity from everyone.

As the CEO, I have high expectations of every individual in that team. I expect every one of them to be as passionate about our organisation as I am – and I am serious about the word passion.

Passion is important because it overcomes the negatives, the challenges, the wearisome long hours, the strenuous efforts. So, to me, passion is an essential ingredient to have in a management team.

As the CEO, I work to empower individual performance. I give our management team my trust, I give them responsibility and I give them accountability and performance indicators.

While I believe you should let managers manage, I find it is also very important that I follow through and be there as a sounding board. I encourage entrepreneurship. I try to ensure they are fulfilling their personal entrepreneurial skills through the organisation. I believe it is important to help them achieve financial security and to help them with their professional, personal and family needs and wants as well.

The other thing, of course, is attitude. You can't beat that. If they don't have the right attitude, they should not be on your management team. I expect my managers to show commitment ... not just of 99 per cent, not 100 per cent, but 110 per cent.

Why do I place such importance on 100 per cent-plus commitment? Because the power of their commitment is going to be transmitted to the next level of managers – and I want them to be stretched as well.

I look to my managers to energise their people through their passion and that commitment. They must have what I call high-tone energy, rather than low-tone energy.

I work to develop my managers by giving them the opportunity and the incentive to grow. I like to see what happens to people after they start with me. Five years down the track I take pride in seeing how my people have evolved and developed on a personal and professional level.

The next thing I expect is health and fitness. In my experience people who are fit have more energy and are better able to cope with the pressure of management roles. So fitness is vitally important.

Once you have got all those qualities in your managers, you can move mountains. When you take them with you to the next level they are excited that they have been challenged and provoked and that they have evolved – and they are looking for fresh challenges. I look to the management team to challenge me as well.

Life is all about evolution. Unless you evolve, you are stagnating and if you have a management made up of stagnant people, you'll find that stagnant will be the word for your company growth as well – and the bottom line will show it.

I believe in complete openness with my management team about the company's financial goals, so I strongly spell them out. I believe that this openness has been a major factor in the success of our organisation.

I think it's very important that you create key performance indicators, or what I call milestones. All of that comes to your vision, your company goal. You tell them what it is you want to achieve and what you are striving for, depending on the department, or depending on the offices, and you empower your managers to execute actions toward your company goals.

But at the same time, it's also very important that you understand the personal and professional goals they themselves hold dear so that there's a double win in the formula of achieving goals.

Goals are something that you have to be able to touch, you have to be able to see. But the most exciting part about reaching a goal is not the actual goal, but the journey to the goal. It's what you become through the journey. It's the experience, the people you meet, the challenges ahead of you, the rejections, the barriers, the tries, and the failures as well as success.

I think it is really important to realise as you're achieving your goal, whether it's a company goal or a personal goal, that you've got to enjoy the journey. Because once you've achieved it, hopefully, you're onto your next goal.

So it's not the goal; it's the joy of the journey to that goal. Once you've achieved the goal you celebrate it. Sometimes (I'm an optimist) I celebrate it in advance. I say 'let's have the champagne in advance because I can already visualise the achievement of the goal'.

And you've got to have fun. That's the other thing. It's so important to not only be passionate and be committed and have that leadership vision and to have the disciplines but you've also got to enjoy and have fun and laugh at yourself. See the funny side of life.

Organisational Performance Management

My policy on performance management through the whole organisation has four prongs to it:

1. Setting clear and convincing short-term and long-term goals;

2. Translating goals into a handful of specific stretch targets for managers;

3. Using benchmarking to prove that a goal is achievable; and

4. Standing back – letting managers manage.

When a business has many parts, as many big businesses do, I believe each office or site should be run as a separate profit centre with the manager having a high level of autonomy and accountability for the performance and achievement of results.

Each office should have a well developed business plan, including business and financial projections and business and promotional strategies, which include achievement of obligations.

I think it's a good idea for a business to provide comprehensive performance reports to all levels of management on a regular basis with details on the achievement of Key Performance Indicators (KPIs) in each office.

The most important question at any time in a business is this: is the business profitable? Are there any black spots? Are any parts of the business losing money? Lots of businesses fail by not knowing the answers until it is too late.

To ensure that everyone is aware of where the business is at any particular time, I recommend that performance reports against the KPIs set for each office be provided to all managers, along with a profit and loss report at the end of each month.

I also recommend that monthly performance be reviewed by the responsible manager together with that manager's senior manager or general manager.

Performance of each division of a business ought to be reviewed in depth on a monthly basis by a General Manager and the CEO.

Business and financial projections need to be re-negotiated and regularly updated.

There needs to be a continuous performance analysis. You need to set benchmarks against your past performances and against other high performers.

Individual performance standards should be set for all staff in discussions between the staff member and the manager. I believe it is important that the staff member be involved in setting goals that are realistic yet challenging.

When a staff member has agreed with a manager that certain standards and goals are attainable I believe an element of pride comes into play that has the effect of boosting the drive of the individual to reach objectives. Of course, the bar should not be set too low – or too high –

but high enough to stretch the individual and to contribute to an improved performance by the office.

It is important that all staff be given regular feedback on their performance by their manager and I believe they should also be given continuous coaching in interpersonal skills and training in job skills. In other words personal development of staff at all levels needs to be encouraged by senior management.

I believe in rewarding good performance. For example, you can award staff bonus payments for those who achieve more than standard results and you can create profit-sharing arrangements for their managers.

High performing staff should be acknowledged and identified in group meetings or in the communications network of the business. In my own case, I make a point of contacting all high performers to thank them and congratulate them for their efforts.

I believe that good communication is the essential element that brings the company's vision to life and ensures that we all drive toward the same goals.

Let me define 'good communication'. I believe you have good communication when:

1.   Everyone understands the goals and targets we're trying to achieve.

2.   Each person understands the part they need to play in achieving these goals;

3.   There are systems and processes to let staff continuously monitor their own and their team performance;

4.   You ensure that discussion about performance is continuous, two-way and constructive;

5.   You encourage people to be open about performance issues;

6.   You treat challenges as opportunities to improve and succeed; and

7.   You celebrate success.

I am constantly on the move, as are my General Managers, visiting all offices throughout institute and our network.

We have a first-name policy for myself, the senior managers and staff at all levels so that everyone will feel relaxed and comfortable enough to raise any issue. In line with my policy of always speaking the truth, the more feedback we get, the better we like it. We want the bad news as well as the good – and if it's bad we do not follow the mediaeval custom of 'shoot the messenger'.

I think it's important that I put my imprint on the personality of the organisation, so I conduct workshops for all staff. It usually takes at least three of these a year to cover all staff.

Training is ongoing. We conduct business improvement workshops for our staff who work in consultant roles in various areas.

I believe staff retention is an essential part of managing for good performance. What a waste it would be to build a successful team and then see it break up for the want of a policy that acknowledges individual needs.

In my career, beginning as an invoice typist, then as a teacher and as an executive in my own growing company, I have learned quite a lot about what people want out of their jobs.

I believe good people – and as I have demonstrated, I only employ the best people – need flexibility and personal empowerment in order to achieve the best results. So in our organisation we give flexibility and empowerment.

While we have quality-assured business procedures, managers and staff have considerable autonomy to identify business opportunities and to implement strategies they believe will achieve required results.

We have no secrets from our staff. They get to know as much as anyone in the management structure about our performance and results. We believe this promotes pride in working for a successful organisation.

As a teacher and as a CEO I am a passionate advocate of personal development. I love to see people grow, so I have put in place a system that offers personal development plans for staff at all levels. In line with this we give staff every opportunity to seek promotion within the company and it is our policy to fill management positions from within the company first, wherever possible.

CHAPTER FOURTEEN

The power of branding

Branding has been a crucial factor in the success of our business. To my family and friends, the words Sarina Russo mean me, the person. But to hundreds of thousands of people across the State of Queensland, Sarina Russo means my business. When they hear the name Russo, they think of education, career training and finding jobs and the same thing is now also happening in NSW and Victoria through the activities of our Sarina Russo Job Access offices.

I have been in the business of brand building for more than 23 years and I can tell you this: the stronger the brand the stronger the business. If you want to grow your business, you must build up your brand.

As I wrote in Chapter Five, when I bought a high-rise building in the heart of Brisbane in 1993 to be my headquarters, I had no false modesty about naming the building after myself.

Until then I had operated my business as 'The Office' Business Academy, but in 1993 it was time to cash in on my public profile. There had been articles in newspapers and magazines for some years about the successes of Sarina Russo, the principal of 'The Office' Business Academy, who worked by the slogans, *how to get that job* and *see you at the top*.

Through those articles and my weekly television spot, *How To Get That Job,* the name Sarina Russo had become associated in the public mind with business and career training and finding jobs. It was time to cement the connection: think training and job-getting; *think Sarina Russo.*

I could see a lot more value in emblazoning my name over that building and our business than by being modest about using it. In fact it would have been stupid to have used another name when I knew my branding was so strong. So what we did was to call the building the Sarina Russo Centre and, over the next few years, the academy became the Russo Institute of Technology.

Under that branding we created a new landmark in the city of Brisbane – and my business grew and grew.

Never under-estimate the value of strong branding. The Internet has made it a more valuable asset than the bottom line of the company. Think about that. We are entering the era of the remote purchase.

When you are surfing the Internet on a shopping expedition, you can't see, touch or smell the items you are thinking about buying. But when you recognise a brand that inspires your trust, a brand that you know because it has been pushed in front of you for years, you are more likely to buy it than an equivalent item that has a brand you have never heard of.

And what a market the internet is. Hundreds of millions of people around the world have Internet access and the numbers are growing year by year. In the next few years the numbers are expected to double.

Consumer spending on retail purchases on the internet is already billions of dollars a year.

The bigger and stronger your brand, the greater your chances of exploiting this huge market. Martha Stewart, whom I discussed in Chapter 11 on corporate ethics, was a branding phenomenon. If a product carried the Martha Stewart brand, it sold.

Until the allegations that she had engaged in insider trading, the US arm of Kmart sold Martha Stewart branded products (everything from Manchester to decorator paints and garden tools) to the value of $US1 billion of every year. The one million or so subscribers to her website sought her advice and bought her products online.

But the insider trading slur turned the market against her. Her brand was blackened and may never recover.

So brand is crucial. Today, any company that launches a product on to the market without sufficient brand development is almost certainly dooming itself to failure. Surveys have shown that a high percentage of new consumer products fail within three years because of poor branding, or because the product is not innovative enough.

So what is brand? I like the following definition I learned during my studies at Harvard: *Brand is a promise between the producer and the customer, over enough time to be believable.*

When branding is really powerful and it's backed up by exceptional product, the consumer is drawn to that brand with the desire to experience an emotional charge.

Why do people buy expensive cars like Porsches and Mercedes? Why do women pay $2000 for a Chanel or Christian Dior handbag? Because they want the emotional rush that comes with possession of the best that there is. When you can afford them, they remind you that you've made it. Celebrate your success.

For $1000 you could buy a truckload of Bic pens, but that's how much, or more, you might pay for a Mont Blanc pen, which is the ultimate in pens. Pulling out that beautiful instrument and working every day with it gives the user a feeling of significance and importance. It's a badge of their success. It's just a pen, but its *the best you can buy* brand that makes them feel terrific.

Such can be the power of branding. Think of the names Versace, Armani, Bvulgari and Giorgio Armani. Their products sell at hugely inflated prices because of their branding.

We all know that Nike sells shoes and sports apparel. We know it by the name Nike and by the swoosh logo that's shaped like a tick. We know it by the 'just do it' mantra that has been adopted into everyday usage. Nike is one of the most powerful brands on earth.

If you don't believe it, just ask a kid who is into sport what he or she would like for Christmas.

Nike started as a company named Blue Ribbon Sports and became Nike in 1978. From that time on, the company went to work building an image around the brand.

Nike's success is proof of that lesson from Harvard: *Brand is a promise between the producer and the customer, over enough time to be believable.*

So if you're starting a business go to work on your brand and make sure it's a promise that is never broken.

CHAPTER FIFTEEN

Winning the customer

You don't have to be a professor of business studies to know that the law of supply and demand no longer operates the way it used to. The supply side of the equation now outweighs the demand side by a huge factor. Catching customers, holding customers is now more difficult than ever before. And it will get worse.

Two things have happened in the last 15 years to make this so: (1) the number of competitors in most product categories has exploded almost beyond belief; and (2) this proliferation in competitors has been further magnified by the increasing rate of technology transfer.

Anything and everything can be copied, or duplicated, with the result that processes which were once proprietary have quickly become widely available. This phenomenon has had another effect, beyond the issue of more competition, in making it more difficult to develop 'ownership' of a customer. The trend toward sameness has blurred the distinctiveness between products which once was the factor that won and held customers.

With technology transference, even when a point of differentiation is achieved, it may not last for long, unless it is a differentiation of a kind that can be continuously worked on to keep it distinctive or unique.

Customers reign supreme in this new, intensively competitive climate. You have to understand that the customers of today are different to those of the 1970s and the 1980s, when it was a sellers' market.

For the reasons outlined above, there is now no guarantee they will repeat their order with you. The challenge in this new millennium is to give customers extra value they can perceive really is extra value. Only then will you have a chance of binding them to you.

How do we give them that perception? My belief is that we have to tell ourselves that customers are just like us. We are consumers, too. We want to feel special, we want to feel significant, we want to feel that we are valued, we want to feel we have done a good deal.

If we can make our customers feel those things, they will want to stay with us and they will be likely to recommend us. Certainly, it takes extra effort to make them feel that way – and maybe extra cost – but I still believe it is cheaper to retain a good customer than to go out and 'buy' a new customer.

There is a rule of thumb that says a happy customer may tell 10 others about what you have to offer. Which is good. An unhappy customer, more ominously, will tell 100 others about the bad experience. Which is very bad. In striving to build that crucial foundation of trust, strive to make your customer happy.

There have been studies which have put a value on customer loyalty. In one study of service firms it was found that extending the customer relationship from five years to six years resulted in a 25 per cent to 85 per cent increase in profitability.

The reason for this was that a long-term customer who becomes knowledgeable about the company and its products is less expensive to serve. As a result, costs are reduced. The word-of-mouth factor also comes into play. By recommending the company to others, the enthusiastic long-term customer generates new business and contributes to increased profitability.

In every business there are different types of customers. There is the easy customer, who is always happy with you. And then there can be the 'difficult' customer, who is always unhappy, no matter what you do.

You should not think of 'difficult' customers as a problem. If you pursue their expectations, they will take your business to another level, the level you achieve through being challenged to do more and give more and raise the bar.

In short, difficult customers present you with the opportunity to make your business better at doing what it does.

Succeeding in business, from my experience, from my observations and from the lessons I have learned, requires that you act with common sense after asking the right questions and putting your finger on simple truths. Don't be distracted from core questions like:

What do our customers really want from our product?

The correct answer is simple: they want it to work for them; they want good value.

Questions like:

What do I have to do to give them what they want?

Again, the correct answer is simple: our product must be readily available, we must make it convenient for them to buy it, it must have functional values that are superior to those of our competitors.

Or, *what do I have to do to make them want to come back?*

The correct answer is simple: we must make their contact with my business an enjoyable experience so that a memorable relationship is created.

You must remember, however, that it will be the customer who will decide how much customer value there is in your product. This is not to say you should not try to influence your customer's perception of value. Rather you should do everything to influence your customer in that perception.

And that brings us to the question of differentiation. Your goal should be to build into your product a difference that makes it more appealing than that of your competitors. If you can succeed in this, not only will you enhance your chances of winning and holding customers, you will be in a powerful position to set the terms of the market.

Take two similar products. Customers will not pay more for one of those two if there is no perceived difference in the two. And why should they? Conversely, if one does have a difference that is perceptible and it enhances the product, the customer will be prepared to pay the higher price.

One of the best lessons I have learned in my business studies at Harvard is this: if the price of a product is less than the perceived value of that product, the customer will buy it and pocket the difference. But if the price is more than the perceived value, the customer will not buy.

Now here's the thing: the seller of a product that has no perceived difference does not set the price. It is the competitor whose product has a perceptible (to the customer) difference that sets the price.

Differentiation, therefore, is a protective mechanism from price competition. The greater the difference the greater the protection.

Our businesses offer services that are widely available in the community. If anyone were to ask me what is the differentiation in the products of our business, I would answer: we have an attitude that builds a strong relationship. Yes, I believe we have more of it than any of our competitors, we work harder on maintaining it than anyone else and we use it more effectively than anyone else.

We make it a live force that powers through our whole organisation. We imbue our customers with it. Our attitude empowers them with the attitude they need to have if they are to graduate with a certificate or diploma, the attitude they need to have if they are to win a job.

We certainly teach skills, but so do other educational institutions and job network organisations like ours. I believe the difference between them and us is our:

Passion

Absolute commitment

Sincerity

Empathy.

It is my belief that people are not going to learn from you if they do not genuinely think you really care about them and the challenges of learning.

I ask my staff to put themselves in the shoes of the students, or the job seekers, or the employers, as I do. In my case, I respond well when I know the professor really cares about me and shows it in his own special way, whether it's extra tutoring or some explanatory notes.

I want everyone in our organisation to be like that professor.

We can count on retaining our customers only if we are **passionate**, only if we always have a caring, can-do **attitude**, only if we are totally **sincere** and only if we deal with our customers with **empathy.**

It comes down to the old saying, 'nobody cares how much you know until they know how much you care'.

I've been out there for more than 23 years of my adult life teaching people and helping them find jobs. And I believe I've done it well. I've taken on every challenge.

I believe everyone who wants to work can go out there and get a job. I really believe that, even if it's self-employment, being a temp, being a casual or a job-share worker. If you want something, you just keep trying until you get what you want. Everyone can go out there and create self-worth. It depends on how much they want it. It depends on their attitude.

We teach that kind of attitude. We are able to get our students and job candidates to believe in it because we have it ourselves. That is our point of differentiation and I believe it is sustainable because we can continuously work on it, strengthen it and improve it.

If a service-oriented business can sustain the right kind of attitude, it has the perfect defence against competition.

This defence is built by avoiding the cycle of mediocrity I explained in Chapter Twelve, *Recruiting the Right People*. The point was that the more your staff were switched on, the greater your customer satisfaction is likely to be.

I see our business process like a pyramid, the ascending tiers of which are:

- Employee capability, which translates as empowerment, or the latitude and ability to deliver results to both internal and external customers.
- Employee satisfaction.
- Employee productivity.
- Employees' ability to deliver good value to customers.
- Customer satisfaction.
- Customer loyalty.

Employee capability is built by hiring the right people, people with attitude, giving them training, support, latitude and rewards. By giving your staff that capability, you are promoting employee satisfaction.

The value of employee satisfaction should not be underrated. Employees who enjoy their work and believe they are making a contribution that is valued, tend to stay longer, become more productive and knowledgeable and create long-term value.

When you have that kind of dynamic going on in your business you are on track to create customer satisfaction. Wouldn't you, as a customer, like to be attended to by someone who is motivated and takes the time to get to know your specific needs and circumstances, someone who makes you feel special?

Of course you would. And so would I. When I am given that kind of treatment I am a happy customer. I'd go back. I'd buy more from them. And I would recommend them to my friends.

And that, in fact, is the way it works. Customer satisfaction can breed customer loyalty and trigger off that valuable word-of-mouth recommendation chain reaction.

And it all comes down to those ascending tiers on the pyramid:

- Employee capability.
- Employee satisfaction.
- Employee productivity.
- Employees' ability to deliver good value to customers.
- Customer satisfaction.
- Customer loyalty.

But if that pyramid is to take your business to the top and to real profitability, every tier on it must be strong. And the only way to build that strength is to work hard on making those first four tiers a real representation of their labels: there must be **real** employee capability, there must be **real** employee satisfaction, there must be **real** employee productivity, there must be **real** employee ability to deliver value to customers with urgency.

You must build it as a culture that is vibrant and strong, permeating the whole organisation from the employee doing the most humble job to the leader at the top. Fairy-dusting the organisation with a 'have a nice day' veneer will not be enough.

Alternative 1

WIN THE CUSTOMER
PYRAMID

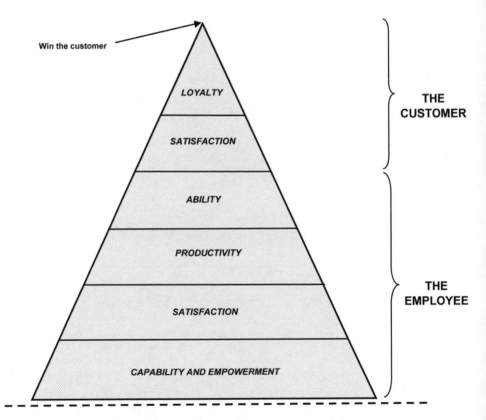

Organisational Culture

CHAPTER SIXTEEN

Sharing the vision of leadership

If there is one thing I have learned in business, it is that as a leader you must have 360-degree vision. Not only do you have a business to run and to grow, you also have a business to protect. In a way, the principles of war apply: you have to patrol the perimeter, watch out for threats. Being in a constant state of alertness and mental readiness to act is essential.

In my process of patrolling the perimeter, I have developed thoughts and opinions on factors that could impinge on our business and the way we do business. I would like to share some of these with you.

First, I would like to discuss uncertainty versus certainty in the 21st century. One of the biggest challenges as a CEO and a leader in business today, particularly since September 11, 2001, is that we are living in a globalised environment in which change is so constant and dramatic that a lot of consumers and a lot of companies lose their way in the speed of that change.

I think one of the greatest books on change is *Who Moved My Cheese?* by Spencer Johnson. It teaches the lesson that in life, in providing for ourselves, there is so much likelihood of unexpected change that, in order to survive, we have to recondition our minds to accept that change is inevitable and we have to shape our lives around acceptance of that inevitability.

One of the things I love about *Who Moved My Cheese?* is that it makes you realise we tend to take too much for granted – our clients, our relationships, our savings, our health. We just think it will always stay the same. And it paints a stark picture of the consequences of thinking that way.

We should not wish for more of the same. We should wish for more of something different, because it prepares us for the uncertainty of a world yet to come.

The world is now dropping its barriers. The challenge in educational institutions and organisations is how do you live with this rapid change? Number One, you have got to prepare yourself with expanded skills and deeper understanding.

There's no point in saying *I've got one great client*, because that great client could just move to another competitor or the government could change and you're left without any business.

So it's very important to patrol the perimeter of your business and keep your mind in a constant state of readiness to act to defend what you've got.

So many of us wish that we won't have to change. We feel comfortable with the environment we're in and we fear that if it changes, when it changes, when our company is re-engineered, we might be re-engineered out.

And let me tell you this: you will be re-engineered out unless you've got the attitude that you want to be, and you're going to be, part of the rapid change, the rapid engineering. There really is no escape. It's happening in companies all over the world.

I guess my advice is that surviving change requires mental preparation, disciplined learning and being curious.

Why is it as children we study ants, and as adults we tread on them? We seem to think we know it all.

Life, even in relationships, is not a guarantee. Nothing has a guarantee any more. Life just keeps changing. One of my favourite songs is *Life Will Never Be The Same* by Haddas. We have to be prepared for change and see it as an opportunity rather than a cause for despair or a crisis.

Why it's so important to anticipate the 'go-wrong' factor

If you're starting a small business, I'll give you a tip. Always make sure your cash flow is healthy. Ensure that you're able to put enough to one side to be able to build a 'bank' for things that may go wrong. You'll find that in any business, there's always the unforeseeable stuff that you never, ever think could happen.

It happened to me in the third year after starting our business. We had a fire. I thought, *well I didn't plan for that*, but fortunately I had accumulated a 'bank' and I was able to move to much better premises that cost 10 times as much, but took the business to greater heights.

Never think that the unforeseeable won't happen to you. Believe me, it will happen. It is how you embrace that inevitability that will govern your future.

You could be the best in the world at what you do, but forces beyond your control, beyond anyone's control, could still damage your business.

The terrible events of September 11 in 2001 are an example. They sent shockwaves around the world. The fear of terrorism brought tourism to a virtual halt. Entire communities that relied on tourism went into painful recession.

Even beyond the tourist-related industries there was a falling off in profits because business confidence and consumer confidence fell to all-time lows.

Here's another example on a different scale. I remember there was a nightclub where the doorman was shot. That nightclub had been doing wonderfully well until that shooting, but after it happened the business died. Everyone had a fear that if you went there, something bad might happen. That was a classic example of an outside influence, which really was out of anyone's control, killing a business.

Always have that 'uncertainty' money to protect yourself against the unforeseeable.

Why I have a policy of buying property

I have a policy of investing in property to protect our business. Maybe this is one of the genes my father passed on to me, because he was a fervent believer in property investment and, as I wrote in Part One of this book, he involved me, when I was still a small child, in the management of the flats he bought for investment.

A lot of people like to have a mixed investment portfolio where they buy shares as well as property. Maybe I don't have enough understanding of shares, but my attitude is that buying shares is a little bit like gambling.

Once you hand over your $10,000 there's no control in the performance of that company. You are trusting and making a judgement of that company's vision and the company's drive to make sure you get your money back plus a little bit more. But as the collapses of companies like HIH, OneTel, Enron and WorldCom have taught us, you can never be sure that what's happening behind the scenes is in your best interests as a shareholder.

As I write this, there has been a crash in the stock market in the US and to a lesser extent in Australia, with many people having the value of their retirement investments slashed.

If you go into property, you can drive past it, you can see it, you can be inspired by it, you can build on it. If you keep it long enough, you will usually find you can double your money or triple it.

My policy is always to look to the assets of property to protect our business, so that when we are doing our Balance Sheet, we've got some true assets in bricks and mortar.

I have a strong philosophy about how you should go about buying property. For example, if you buy a house, you know you've done a great deal when you're certain you could sell it at a profit the same day you bought it.

I think sometimes you get confused in saying, well one day it's going to be worth 'x'. Instead, negotiate hard so that the piece of real estate you have bought has got an immediate profit value the day your purchase is settled.

I am not suggesting you should do as I do. Everyone is different. There is a sound rule of investment that you should never put all of your eggs in one basket. It's smart to diversify your investment portfolio. I achieve diversification through my businesses, to which my property investments are an adjunct.

My advice to others is: do what's best for you. Use your emotional intelligence and take investment advice from professionals.

Why you must strategise your business

Now let's talk about strategy. How important is it to strategise your leadership, your vision and to empower management to execute that vision? It's super important, as my time at Harvard has emphasised.

Strategy, in my terms, is where you have a sit-down discussion with your management team to hammer out an understanding of where you would like to take your company, and go through all the associated issues like how will we achieve the growth we seek? Where will the growth lead to? How much is it going to cost? What's the consumer going to want? Will it fill the consumers' needs? And so on.

Once upon a time, the gurus of business used to strategise five years out from now, ten years out from now. In this new, changing and uncertain world, it is still important to set a long-term strategy but because so much change is happening it is now equally important to strategise on a weekly, monthly and yearly basis.

It's important to believe in the corporate value of strategising. I think of strategy as being the agent of change that gives you a vision, like an architect. When he builds a house, the architect knows exactly where the fireplace is going to be.

An architect can actually take you to an empty block of land and say, *Sarina you've just bumped into the fireplace*. He knows exactly where it's going to be.

Strategy is like a business architect who is precisely plotting what steps and actions are going to be executed to be able to achieve your objectives in a business. You are able to know exactly what is in your mind before you start it.

That's also the power of visualisation, seeing something complete before you actually get it started. Unless you visualise it in your mind and on paper, it's hard to communicate your thoughts and spell out the 'how to' part of strategising.

In my studies at the Harvard Business School, in 2002, we were lectured on corporate strategy, which is now seen as one of the most pressing (and neglected) issues for modern business. There are two aspects to strategy – **business level strategy** or how to build a sustainable competitive advantage in a discrete and identifiable market, and **corporate level strategy**, which is the overall plan for a diversified company.

We were introduced to a new definition of corporate strategy as being: *'The way a company creates value through the configuration and co-ordination of its multi-market activities'.*

There are three aspects to this definition. First is the emphasis on value creation as the ultimate purpose of corporate strategy. The second is the focus on the multi-market scope of the company, or its configuration. The third is how the company manages the business activities of its various components.

It was stressed that having a well-conceived corporate strategy was as important to a small business as it was to a large one. What it ultimately comes to is this: the focus of a corporate strategy is on the relationship between the whole firm and the individual parts of the firm. The test of the value of a corporate strategy is whether it makes individual business units better or worse by their presence in the corporation.

The value of an effective corporate strategy will ultimately be realised in the business units through their enhanced ability to deliver goods and services to customers.

You can strategise your business plan, you can have a marketing strategy, you can have a human resources strategy, you can have an investment strategy. There are so many facets of strategy today, but in my view none is more important than competitive strategy.

Why competitive strategy is so important to a business

You must have a strategy to deal with competition and it should be put together in blueprint form.

As a leader, I think it is crucially important that you share with your management and your people that competition is real – and it is normal. Sometimes I go into management meetings where they say, *'the reason we haven't done well is because we've got increased competition in this product'.*

When they say that to me, I immediately reply, *'what else do you have as your excuse, because competition has been existing since day one of our business'.*

It is normal that competitors are going to try to emulate the market leader. I know we do it. We go looking for the best and emulate the best.

The thing is, in the 21st Century, we can all emulate, so what can you do to stay ahead of the competition? The answer is to make the speed of your delivery the point of difference.

By speed of delivery I do not mean getting product out faster to the market. I mean it as finding a way to identify and fulfil the wants and needs of your customers faster than anyone else. You discover what their tastes are, ahead of your competition, and you go about fulfilling their tastes before your rivals do.

To do this you must engage in effective market research and your whole operation must be in sync. Your staff must have the capability factor, the empowerment I wrote about in earlier chapters on recruitment and winning the customer, so that your total business is focused not just on service but on customer value and customer satisfaction.

One of the great gurus of competitive strategy is Michael Porter, the associate professor of business administration at the Harvard Business School, where he created a course entitled, Industry and Competitive Analysis.

In his teachings, one of the examples he gives of competitive strategy is of a soap company that entered the market that was dominated by well-entrenched giants like Palmolive and won itself a significant market share by differentiating their product as being not just soap, but also as an anti-bacterial treatment for the skin ... *it's not just a soap that washes your skin but it also enhances and protects your skin,* was the strategy. The product was Neutragena.

With this differentiation factor goes the need to train your team to understand exactly what that differentiation is. Unless they know it all, unless they believe it all, unless they can explain it with passion and commitment, it's very hard to sell the right perception of the product to the consumers.

The other thing is branding. It's so important to compete on branding. This is why many companies are spending more and more money on their branding, which is another form of competitive differentiation.

Why you need to know how to
manage a business slow-down

Sometimes we are confronted with a slow-down of business. Now this could be as a result of the economy, although I never, ever use that as an excuse. Or it could be that the product has changed, or the service is no longer required or there's a newly elected government, or a new product has superseded the old one.

There can be many causes, but the most fundamental thing for a CEO is to have a mindset that can deal with a slow-down without getting rattled.

To me, a slow-down is an opportunity to assess your product or to assess your service and to understand what it is in the market place that has changed, or is in the process of change.

It's an opportunity to revive, to renew, to re-engineer and it may mean you have to look within as well as outside, especially in an organisation like mine. What you need to do is embrace the slowdown as if it is, right now, an opportunity for you to develop, research, restructure and prepare for a major turn-around in your business.

To survive these slow-down periods you must imbue your business with a positive attitude. What you need to do as a leader is to make sure that a slow-down doesn't create complacency among the staff. You must still create the urgency. You must ensure that the urgency of delivery, the speed, the dynamics, the chemistry, the synergy doesn't go because your customers are always alert to signals of negative change and may turn to your competitors.

If you become sluggish in a slow-down, it's dangerous. You've got to take the pace faster, smarter, harder and drive it more than when it's in peak mode. You've got to plan ahead, because the causes of the downturn will eventually clear away and when they do, you should have put the business in a position to achieve renewed growth.

Why complacency is the greatest enemy a business can face

Complacency is the greatest enemy a business can face. When it infects a business, that business will fall behind change rather than lead it.

To combat complacency, you must raise the urgency-level within the company. A good leader constantly drives the organisation with an urgency versus complacency policy.

There are ways to do this, like:

- Identifying/focusing on a financial loss, exposing managers to major weaknesses in relation to their competitors.
- Cutting the fat (looking at operational expenses).
- Setting stretch targets.
- Putting more accountability on individuals.
- Sending out more data about customer satisfaction.

Combat Complacency
Create Urgency

- Sending out more data on financial performance.

- Sending out more information that demonstrates weakness in your company in relation to your competitors.

- Insisting that staff talk regularly to unsatisfied customers and unhappy suppliers.

- Challenging your team.

- Leaving off the gloss and speaking the truth in staff communications.

- Inspiring your staff with visions of the rewards of great achievements.

Why I believe in the power of networking

For any one, at any level in business, it is helpful to be able to share your frustrations, experiences or concerns with people on a similar level. In other words it's great to be in a network of people who will understand what you're going through.

A great thing happened to me when I was nominated as the first Queensland woman of the Australian chapter of the international Young Presidents' Organisation. The YPO has been a wonderful networking organisation for me, not just domestically but also nationally, and internationally as well.

I think it is extremely important to develop a networking stream in your business and to participate in your community associations, whatever they may be.

It's also helpful to become interested in politics. You don't have to join a party, but you owe it to yourself to stay in touch with the various policies and personalities. In my case I give support to those people, regardless of their political alignment, whom I think are likely to make the greatest contribution to the betterment of society.

The value to me is that I come into contact with the key people in those parties and get an insight into the way they are thinking.

I think, as a business leader, you owe it to the community or you owe it to your organisation to be actively interested in what's happening in your city, state and country and internationally.

The other thing is, networking is really all about building relationships where you find a common interest in a particular niche market and you develop a relationship.

Another thing I think is really valuable is writing three 'thank you' letters every day, or cutting out an article and sending it to a client who maybe is interested in the same issue.

I like to stay in touch, communicate with my network, send emails, make phone calls, send out Christmas cards, invite someone to a particular seminar they may be interested in ... organise an invitation to my place, or say I'm going past and would like to drop in.

Guys can go to their men's clubs and women should have the same sort of opportunity. Women who were at the frontiers 10 years ago, 20 years ago, achieved so many breakthroughs in society. I remember when I went for my first housing loan in 1976, I was told by a bank manager that they didn't lend to women.

I walked out of there aghast that just by being a woman, I was disqualified. Today, however, I find that banks treat women equally.

Opportunities have opened up in politics, in government and in public company boards of directors for women to demonstrate their talent. I have many opportunities to work on boards. I really believe women today have great opportunities to become independent. They may have to work harder than a man to achieve recognition, but this gives them the opportunity to walk away with more skills, more confidence, more self-esteem, a better self-image, greater freedom and more security.

I like to encourage the belief that security is not money. Security is you.

Why constant communication is crucial

Communication is the key to progress and growth in a business or in a personal relationship. It can either break or enhance a relationship.

If you look at a personal relationship – and let's go to 'personal' because it's a great learning curve – sometimes it breaks down because you stop talking to that loved one. You don't want to communicate with them.

I can be a culprit of that. I think ... *they should know how I feel.* Or ... *they should understand the situation.* Or they should...

But there is no 'should' in our life. It is a choice.

Now let's turn to business. There are many ways of communicating to your consumers the information you want them to know about your products.

I use television, radio, newspapers and the Internet, but my prime objective is to tap into the greatest advertising medium of them all: word-of-mouth.

Television has been a great way of sending out a strong message about our product and services.

I also use radio because people can actually hear my message re-stated and re-statement can be a powerful force in attracting business.

Of course, today we have got the web page, the Internet tool, where you can just go to your computer and search for a product or a service. My web page is called *www.sarinarussogroup.com.au.*

The newspaper provides another strong endorsement in communicating to consumers.

But the most powerful force of all is word-of-mouth. Nothing is better than when you get that chain reaction going of people saying good things about your product or service.

When that message catches on and runs through the community, you've got it made.

In terms of internal communication, I'm a great believer in meeting people face-to-face. I like to communicate one on one, visiting our office sites.

As I mentioned earlier I send out a weekly email entitled *from Sarina Russo's desk* to everyone in the organisation. In it I talk about what's happening in the business and what I'm planning to do and so on.

I also communicate internally and externally through brochures, standard newsletters and newsletters on the Internet.

Unless you communicate on a constant basis, people do forget. There is so much happening in our lives that unless you are constantly in people's faces, they will go elsewhere, because they have forgotten. They can forget within 24 hours.

Our business is not only a relationship business but it is also a business in which one must constantly communicate the values of our product and our services.

Why I believe emotional intelligence is a powerful tool

I have made some of my biggest decisions by using intuition, which men call gut feeling. I believe women have a more acute sense of intuition then men and they use it better.

It has been suggested that women developed intuition as an extra protective sense because they were physically weaker than men. By 'intuiting' what these physically stronger creatures were likely to do, they could protect themselves.

This form of intuition apparently enabled them to 'read' men's intentions. For example, they would know if a man was lying by certain subtle signals he was giving out.

I can believe this. Women are far more observant than men. They see the details of things, whereas men generally tend to see the whole and not the fine detail. Ask a man to find something in a cupboard and he'll call on a woman for help to locate it. Ask any wife whether this is true.

Let me share a story with you. Some seven or eight years ago Len Slazenger, who was a Professor at the Harvard Business School, came to Brisbane to speak to a Young Presidents' Association group.

We were talking about the tools of business. I was the only female in the room and I stood up and said, 'well the difference between women and men is intuition. We females have intuition.'

I can tell you there was a roar of laughter from every guy at the seminar. I was so embarrassed. They made me feel as if I was an idiot because I stood up and said that intuition was something that women do have.

Today, the word *intuition* has been linked to what is described as emotional intelligence, a faculty much to be desired in business leaders and executives.

It's now been established in studies that the _most effective_ leaders are alike in one crucial way: they all have a high degree of emotional intelligence.

Emotional intelligence has been defined as the capacity for recognising our feelings and those of others, for motivating ourselves, and managing emotions in us and in our relationships.

There are said to be five components of emotional intelligence – first and foremost self-awareness, or the ability to recognise and understand your moods, emotions and drives as well as their effect on others. The other four are self-regulation, motivation, empathy and social skill.

Sometimes you make a decision and you don't have the facts and figures, but it just 'feels right'. Sometimes I can look at the facts, I can look at the figures, and I'll think, 'no, I shouldn't really go ahead with this.'

I would say that 99 per cent of the time when I have made decisions on my intuitive intelligence, I've been very happy with the decision.

I think you'll find in the 21st century, more and more women are going to surpass men because of this incredible natural business tool called 'intuition' and emotional intelligence.

Science will show that it's a real business tool and one that will be envied by males. And that's not for one moment saying we're smarter. It's just saying we women have a sixth sense called intuition or emotional intelligence.

I believe men can acquire it – I know men who use it. They have mastered it by changing their habits. As a rule, it doesn't come naturally with the male species.

Think global but act local

What's going on in the world right now is a process called the Third Industrial Revolution, which is a product of two forces: information technology and globalisation.

Globalisation is the removal of market or other barriers to create a single market or a single zone. It is the destruction of walls both political and geographical. It involves all aspects of life including commerce, education, politics, trade, manufacturing services. It is also responsible for the decentralisation of business.

Information technology (the Internet) is the most critical driving force of the Third Industrial Revolution. Advances in information technology and the Internet allow:

- Greater processing power, thus replacing low-skilled labour;
- Business and people to interconnect globally with ease.

This promotes commerce, education, interaction, participation and many other aspects of life.

Globalisation increases competition and draws even greater demands from companies and their employees. Accordingly, employees must become more skilled in knowledge-based products and services rather than specialisation in physical-based activities.

So what is likely to be the time lag for the Third Industrial Revolution to make it a better world for business and consumers?

One estimate I have read says that the time lag between the introduction of major technological change and the payoff in higher productivity – and hence general well-being – could be about 20 years.

Given that 20 years have already elapsed since the start of the computer revolution, we seem to be poised at that point of time when it is all going to come together and change our lives in extraordinary ways.

As a disciple of change, I see a whole new exciting world ahead for all of us. My advice is: look for opportunities, for I am sure there will be many.

CHAPTER SEVENTEEN

Negotiating a deal

There are two golden rules for negotiating a deal. The first is: be prepared to accept the worst; and the second is, know who you are negotiating with. Both require elaboration. Let's talk about the first.

When I say be prepared to accept the worst, I mean you should know in your heart what is the worst thing that can happen if you negotiate hard. For example if you are negotiating to buy a property, I guess the worst result would be that the price you have set as your best offer is rejected.

So you don't get the house. Can you live with that? Can you carry the attitude, *well if I don't get this one, there is always another house?* If you can't, you'll find your negotiations become weak. But if you can live with it ... ah, there's a different story. You won't be intimidated. You will be strong. You will put your offer on the table with a take it or leave it attitude that will throw the doubt to the other side, who will be thinking *... this person seems so sure about the value of this property ... can we hope to get a better offer elsewhere?*

My brother-in-law Gerardo Pennisi is a great example of how to do a deal. Here's how he handles our property negotiations. He does the due diligence on the property, satisfies himself that it meets our specifications and goes in with an offer to buy it on the spot: no conditions about

195

engineers' reports or availability of finance. An absolutely unconditional offer. Just, we'll take it at this price, right now. Take it, or leave it.

Of course the price is probably below the market value, and usually below offers other potential purchasers have made (usually with conditions), but Gerry always has a sweetener – a cheque in his pocket to seal the deal right there and then. That cheque is always for an amount two or three times higher than the amount the vendors would normally expect to be paid as a deposit.

He's making the deal look easy. No bickering, no protracted negotiations and real money on the table. And it usually works ... I guess because we've all been conditioned by that old adage, a bird in the hand is worth two in the bush.

One of the people I think about when I talk about negotiating a deal is Donald Trump, the tycoon of real estate in New York. He wrote a book called *The Negotiations of the Deal,* in which he says: '*I always go into a deal accepting that I can live with the worst and the good will take care of itself.*'

I think they are powerful words. Whether you are negotiating over a piece of real estate, or you're in a job interview, or you're going for a loan from a bank – or bidding for a contract – you will always put your case more strongly, more passionately and with more determination and focus if you are not intimidated by the fear of not pulling it off.

When I say *know who you are negotiating with,* I mean you must know whether the person on the other side of the table has the full authority to make a decision, or is just an intermediary.

When you are dealing with the person who has the power to sign the deal you have the power to walk away because there is no strategy to pull you into negotiations (combat) with a fresh adversary. You know that all of your reasoning is getting through to the decision maker and your key points will not be lost in the translation by a subordinate to a superior.

Furthermore, you are less likely to have disputes or confusion about the interpretation of a particular provision; and you will have created a relationship that may bring benefits down the track.

Using property negotiations as an example, I believe it is the real estate agent's job to introduce you to the owner and then to step back to let you negotiate with the owner. Of course that's not the way most agents like to do things, but in my experience from a buying perspective, it is to your advantage to have that direct contact with the owner.

The need to negotiate arises when you don't have the power to achieve or force a certain outcome or behaviour. Your alternative then is to negotiate in order to _influence_ that outcome or behaviour.

You go into the negotiation because you believe it is to your advantage to do so, but a negotiated solution will be to your advantage only if you don't have a better option. To be successful the negotiations must be built on a framework that is based on each side knowing:

- what is the best alternative to a negotiated deal;
- what is the minimum threshold for a negotiated deal;
- how flexible they are willing to be; and
- precisely what tradeoffs are they prepared to make?

Of course, you have more power in a negotiation when you have a good best alternative and the other side does not. It's as simple as that.

And if that situation is reversed, your remaining option is to follow golden rule No. 1: be prepared to accept the worst, which means going into the negotiation with all of your passion and determination – without fear.

Attitude and confidence are not just important characteristics to have. They are crucial. They are everything. They make winners.

CHAPTER EIGHTEEN

Good health creates wealth

To succeed at any level in business you must be reasonably fit in your body and balanced in your mind. You need body fitness for energy and endurance. And as a leader you certainly need plenty of those qualities. You need mind-balance to be able to cope with the mixture of positive and negative forces that will come at you. As a leader you need a lot of that – more so, in fact, than anyone down the line.

Neither physical fitness nor mind balance will come to you as natural gifts. You have to work at both. Fitness, of course, comes from exercise and diet. Mind balance comes from offsetting your work stresses with relaxation through recreation and socialising and by taking well constructed breaks from your work environment.

I do not smoke and if I drink alcohol, it will be only a glass or two of a quality wine or champagne. And I've given up coffee.

Working at my fitness and on my mind balance are key aspects of my life routine. In my pursuit of fitness, I follow the dictum I have already mentioned in this book, *the pain of discipline weighs ounces – the pain of regret weighs tons.*

This means I get out and do it, jogging, walking or swimming. I have no sympathy for people who fall by the wayside. If they want to get into the game of career development – and get ahead of the game – they must realise ... *if it is to be, it's up to me.*

You've just got to get up off that chair or out of that bed and go do it. It's easy to make excuses and not go out and do that walk, that run, that swim or that bike ride. But the kick you will get from the achievement outweighs the negatives – the benefits are enormous. We may look out the window at 5.30 or 6 a.m. and feel it's so cold out there, so lonely, so wet and so miserable, you may say to yourself *I'll do it tomorrow when the weather is better.*

You can lie in bed feeling that the mind wants to, but the body can't get up and get out there, but it can! Believe me, I've had those mornings. I know the struggle. You'll find it easier to conquer that early morning reluctance if you've got a deal going with a friend to work out together. Or hire a fitness coach.

Let me tell you how I overcome it. I start thinking about how I will feel AFTER I've done that run or that swim. I know my body is going to sing, I am going to feel terrific, empowered to launch into the day. I can't wait to win that feeling. And that's what gets me going.

When you're working under a lot of pressure, as I am, you need to learn to read your body for signs of stress and you need to develop techniques to calm you down when you begin to feel them. I have two that serve me well.

If I'm in a situation that is heading toward being stressful, I will listen to my breathing. If it is shallow and rapid, which is a sure sign of acute stress, I will start taking a few slow, deep breaths all the while telling myself to relax. The act of taking those slow, deep breaths does have a soothing affect and it also gives you inner focus. I guess that's why elite athletes do it before launching themselves into a race or a performance: they're getting that inner focus and marshalling their strength.

The other technique is to take a walk. Do you know that walking is not only good exercise, and good for the physiology of the body, it also cheers you up and relaxes you? A German study of people suffering from depression determined that walking was more beneficial than anti-depressant drugs.

Researchers at the Freie University of Berlin put 12 depression sufferers through a program of walking for half an hour a day on a treadmill and increased their workout as their fitness levels rose. After only 10 days, six patients were much less depressed, including five who had been resistant to drug treatment.

In a situation of stress I'm not saying you should take off on a long hike, but a nice brisk walk outside for five or 10 minutes will burn off excess nervous energy and clear your mind. In fact you're likely to return from your walk with a simple solution to whatever the problem was that was causing the stress.

Watching your diet is another important part of staying strong. Don't over-eat and don't starve yourself either. Avoid junk food. Tune your body with a diet that is high in vegetables, fruits, grains and lean protein. I like to go to Japanese restaurants because they serve foods that fit into that category. I avoid drinking a lot of tea and as I said I have given up coffee. I follow the advice of nutritionists and fitness advisers and drink lots of water.

My days are often long and hectic, dealing with people at all levels inside and outside my business. I need to have a lot of nervous energy to keep going. I love my life, so it's easy to overdo things. But, again by listening to my body, I know when I have to recharge my batteries. When I get that feeling, I'll work my schedule so that I can take a morning off to sleep-in, get a couple of hours extra sleep. Then I'll have a massage, listen to music, read something interesting and remote from work, make a few phone calls to friends, maybe go out to lunch with someone who is amusing, relaxing company and check by the office in the early afternoon.

At weekends, I will catch up with my family and friends or get into the countryside or to the beach.

I do these things because it is important to have balance in your life. You must have a life away from work, otherwise you will burn out.

I have made another discovery about running a business that has made a big difference to my life – and to my business. It concerns that age-old debate about whether a business owner, the person who holds the ultimate responsibility for the organisation's continued vitality or demise, can be spared for a few weeks (or months) in order to take a sabbatical.

I have proved the affirmative. I do take a sabbatical every year. Each time, I come back refreshed and empowered by new knowledge and the wider vision I have acquired. During my absence, key people in my business take on greater responsibilities and expand their skills in a way that would not have happened if I had not taken a sabbatical.

In the year 2001 I went to Venice to attend business seminars presented by the Young Presidents' Organisation. It's an annual event and these seminar sessions are called a university. Joining in with other young CEOs from around the world in these university discussions and briefings is a fantastic, stimulating experience.

I find that the experience of getting into mind sessions with other business leaders tests my business know-how and affirms my skills.

In 2002 I also did a lot of travelling as described in Chapter Seven.

Ten years ago when I began making annual visits to the Harvard Business School, I re-learned the importance of asking big picture questions such as, *what are we doing here, and why?*

Each time I return from my annual sabbatical, I bring back an objective view of my own business and this is the true value of the experience. When you are buried neck-deep in a business, glued to a fixed routine, it's virtually impossible to step back and take an objective view.

But getting that objective view is crucial to the success of your business. I can link the milestones in the growth and the success of my business to the new insights I have gained from my annual breaks at Harvard and YPO universities and to the 'refreshed' objective view I have come back with each time.

For some years now I have been convening my management team at least once a year to create a situation in which each of them is able to take an objective view of where we are going, what we are doing and answering questions like are they taking advantage of changes in the business and are they staying true to their mission?

It's simple as this: for your own good, for the good of your business, it's just as important to know when to let go as it is to know when to hold on. If you think your business will fail unless you are there at all times, you haven't created a business, you have built yourself a prison.

Epilogue

As the reader will have gathered, my father had an enormous influence on my life. He was the young Sicilian farmer who left his impoverished home village of Castiglione as a 38-year-old in 1952 to migrate to Australia.

He left behind a wife and four children. I was the youngest, a babe-in-arms. He wanted more for his family than was available in Castiglione. He was going to build a future for them in the faraway land of Australia.

It took him four years of working as a road maker, bridge builder and sharefarmer to scrape together enough money to bring his family to Australia to join him in the humble house he had bought in Wickham Terrace, Brisbane.

As I grew up, learning the nuances of the English language he found impossible to master, I became his assistant in the business ventures he entered into by investing the family fund of money we accumulated by working, every one of us, seven days a week.

There were flats (apartments) and a vineyard. I was his spokesperson in renting out the flats, selling the produce from the vineyard, completing his annual tax return.

I was lucky. I was the child asking the questions put into my mind by a wise man whose only handicap was that he could not speak the language fluently. The questions were his questions and as those very smart, very pertinent questions funnelled through me and the answers came back through me, I acquired attitudes that were older than my years.

I became streetwise. Everything I am today I owe to the apprenticeship I learned at my father's side. I learned how to ask the right questions, I learned how to process the answers, I acquired a thirst for knowledge and an instinct for reading human nature, and I developed a driving ambition to build something that would give me and my family financial independence.

In 2001, when I travelled to Italy for the Young Presidents' Organisation seminars in Venice, I took time out to visit Sicily and my mother and father's home village of Castiglione, the place of my birth. The emotion of meeting my cousins in this impoverished little village, where 80 per cent of the people have no jobs or are retired, had me in tears all day.

In memory of my mother and father, I hired a whole restaurant and put on a feast for 50 of my close relatives, mostly cousins. We had music and dancing and singing and laughter, hugs and kisses, stories and tears. It was wonderful.

I visited them all in their homes – such humble dwellings, but so full of happiness.

Through my devotion to my business, I had left them behind. I had not been back in 18 years. But this time, before I left Castiglione, I made a pledge to each and every one of them: '*I will never leave you behind again. From this day forward, you will be part of my life.*'

I made a commitment to start a scholarship program for all the sons and daughters of my first cousins, 20 of them. I am bringing them to Australia and giving them a year of English and business classes at the Russo Institute of Technology after which they may return to Italy to pursue careers.

I am doing this in the memory of my father Antonino, that brave young man who sailed away from Sicily half a century ago to find fortune for his family. If it were not for him, and if it were not for my darling mother, his loyal, hard-working wife, and my sisters and brother, I would never have been where I am today.

It is time to give something back to my heritage. It is time to say, Antonino Russo, thank you for your courage, thank you for your example, thank you for your vision, thank you for my life.

I dedicate these scholarships to you.

Postscript

As I began work on this book in 2001, I was thinking about buying a high rise building in the heart of the city of Brisbane in Queen Street, which is known as the 'Big End' of town.

I made a pledge to myself then that before I finished the book I would buy that building, my third in the heart of the city. Acquiring it, would take me to the next step on the pathway to establishing the Russo Private University, offering courses that will enable young people and mature age students from around the world to realise their dreams of building successful careers.

The words I live by are: *it can be done!*

And I can say, it has been done. I bought the building. It happened on a Friday night. The negotiators for the vendors were reluctant to sign a contract right then. They suggested I should take the weekend to read through the details of the contract. I declined.

I didn't want to leave any room for slips-ups, or another buyer coming out of the woodwork with a better offer. I followed my rule of striking while the iron is hot.

We used my brother-in-law Gerardo's strategy of making an unconditional offer, backed up by a sizeable deposit cheque. Once again, it worked. The building is ours.

It has become the national headquarters of Sarina Russo Job Access (Australia) and we've named it The Sarina Russo Plaza.

So *it can be done.*

Ciao for now. See you at the top!